MARINE SCIENCE

The People Behind the Science

KATHERINE CULLEN, PH.D.

CHELSEA HOUSE
PUBLISHERS
An imprint of Infobase Publishing

Marine Science: The People Behind the Science

Chelsea House
An imprint of Infobase Publishing
132 West 31st Street
New York NY 10001

Library of Congress Cataloging-in-Publication Data

Cullen, Katherine E.
    Marine science : the people behind the science / Katherine Cullen.
      p. cm.—(Pioneers in science)
    Includes bibliographical references and index.
    ISBN 0-8160-5465-7 (hardcover : acid-free paper)
    1. Marine scientists—Biography. 2. Marine sciences—History. I. Title.
II. Series.
    GC30.A1.C85 2005
    551.46'092'2—dc22   2004030237

Text design by Mary Susan Ryan-Flynn
Cover design by Cathy Rincon
Illustrations by Bobbi McCutcheon

Printed in the United States of America

MP FOF 10 9 8 7 6 5 4 3 2 1

This book is printed on acid-free paper.

*I dedicate this book to
all future pioneers in science.*

CONTENTS

PREFACE

Being first in line earns a devoted fan the best seat in the stadium. The first runner to break the ribbon spanning the finish line receives a gold medal. The firstborn child inherits the royal throne. Certain advantages or privileges often accompany being the first, but sometimes the price paid is considerable. Neil Armstrong, the first man to walk on the Moon, began flying lessons at age 16, toiled at numerous jobs to pay tuition, studied diligently to earn his bachelor's degree in aerospace engineering, flew 78 combat missions in Korea as a brave navy pilot, worked as a civilian test pilot for seven years, then as an astronaut for NASA for another seven years, and made several dangerous trips into space before the historic *Apollo 11* mission. He endured rigorous physical and mental preparation, underwent years of training, and risked his life to courageously step foot where no man had ever walked before. Armstrong was a pioneer of space exploration; he opened up the way for others to follow. Not all pioneering activities may be as perilous as space exploration. But like the ardent fan, a pioneer in science must be dedicated; like the competitive runner, she must be committed; and like being born to royalty, sometimes providence plays a role.

Science encompasses all knowledge based on general truths or observed facts. More narrowly defined, science refers to a branch of knowledge that specifically deals with the natural world and its laws. Philosophically described, science is an endeavor, a search for truth, a way of knowing, or a means of discovering. Scientists gain information through employing a procedure called the scientific method. The scientific method requires one to state the problem and formulate a testable hypothesis or educated guess to describe a phenomenon or explain an observation, test the hypothesis experimentally or by collecting data from observations, and draw conclusions from the results. Data can eliminate a hypothesis, but never confirm it with absolute certainty; scientists may accept a hypothesis as true when sufficient supporting evidence has been obtained. The process sounds entirely straightforward, but sometimes advancements in science do not follow such a logical approach. Because humans make the observations, generate the hypothesis, carry out the experiments, and draw the conclusions, students of science must recognize the personal dimension of science.

Pioneers in Science is a set of volumes that profile the people behind the science, individuals who initiated new lines of thought or research. They risked possible failure and often faced opposition but persisted to pave new pathways of scientific exploration. Their backgrounds vary tremendously; some never graduated from secondary school, while others earned multiple advanced degrees. Familial affluence allowed some to pursue research unhindered by financial concerns, but others were so poor they suffered from malnutrition or became homeless. Personalities ranged from exuberant to somber and gentle to stubborn, but they all sacrificed, giving their time, insight, and commitment because they believed in the pursuit of knowledge. The desire to understand kept them going when they faced difficulties, and their contributions moved science forward.

The set consists of eight separate volumes: *Biology; Chemistry; Earth Science; Marine Science; Physics; Science, Technology, and Society; Space and Astronomy;* and *Weather and Climate.* Each book contains 10 biographical sketches of pioneering individuals in a subject, including information about their childhood, how they entered into their scientific careers, their research, and enough background science information for the reader to appreciate their discoveries and contributions. Though all the profiled individuals are certainly distinguished, their inclusion is not intended to imply that they are the greatest scientists of all time. Rather, the profiled individuals were selected to reflect a variety of subdisciplines in each field, different histories, alternative approaches to science, and diverse characters.

Each chapter includes a chronology and a list of specific references about the individual and his work. Each book also includes an introduction to the field of science to which its pioneers contributed, line illustrations, photographs, a glossary of scientific terms related to the research described in the text, and a listing of further resources for information about the general subject matter.

The goal of this set is to provide, at an appropriate level, factual information about pioneering scientists. The authors hope that readers will be inspired to achieve greatness themselves, to feel connected to the people behind science, and to believe that they may have a positive and enduring impact on society.

ACKNOWLEDGMENTS

I would like to thank Frank K. Darmstadt, Executive Editor of science and mathematics at Infobase Publishing, for his skillful guidance and extreme patience, and to Melissa Cullen-DuPont, for having all the answers. Appreciation is also extended to illustrator Bobbi McCutcheon for her dedicated professionalism and to Amy L. Conver and Ann E. Hicks for their constructive suggestions. The reference librarians and support staff of the main branch of the Medina County District Library, located in Medina, Ohio, deserve acknowledgment for their assistance in obtaining interlibrary loans, acquiring numerous special requests, and handling the hundreds of materials and resources the author borrowed during the writing of this set. Gratitude is also expressed to Pam Shirk, former media specialist at A. I. Root Middle School in Medina, Ohio, for sharing her expertise. Many people and organizations generously gave permission to use their photographs. Their names are acknowledged underneath the donated images. Thank you all.

INTRODUCTION

Water covers more than 71 percent of the surface of the Earth, giving it the nickname "the blue planet." More than 90 percent of the Earth's living space is in the ocean, and until 500 million years ago, all life-forms existed there. The health of the planet and its inhabitants depends on the cycling of water and the minerals and nutrients it carries. For millions of years, the oceans have influenced climate and weather patterns. Human's relationship with the sea began in ancient times as he depended on it for food, livelihood, and enjoyment, but lack of technology limited the ability of people to explore the oceans scientifically until recently. In addition to numerous economically valuable resources acquired from the seas, scientists have found insight into the origin of life, model organisms for studying reproduction and development, and geological processes at work shaping the Earth.

Early marine studies involved pulling nets through the water behind a boat or dragging buckets of mud from the seafloor to the surface. Introduced in the early 1700s, the diving bell, a large container that was open at the bottom and filled with air supplied from leather tubes, allowed men to work in shallow water for short periods of time. A century later, diving suits that were connected via hoses to an air supply aboard a ship increased the mobility of a submerged person. In the 1940s, the introduction of scuba gear freed divers from the restrictions of any cable, allowing horizontal and vertical movement within a safe range of depths. Because water pressure on the body increases with depth, divers whose bodies were not protected in an enclosed, pressure-controlled environment could only descend about 100 feet (30 m). When submersible vehicles, such as the bathysphere and bathyscaph, allowed men to dive much deeper, explorers were amazed at the previously unseen colorful scenery and abundance of interesting organisms. Today, from the safety of a research vessel, scientists skillfully maneuver remote-controlled robots that have real-time video capabilities for recording observations and coordinated mechanical arms for recovering samples from the bottom of the ocean floor. Sonar reveals information about the seabed, and photographs taken from satellites in space expose marine geological formations.

The marine sciences include all of the sciences as they relate to the sea. For example, *marine biology* is the study of organisms that live in the sea; a marine biologist might examine the distribution of populations in different zones due to different temperatures or light requirements. A chemist might study the composition of seawater with respect to its salinity and dissolved gases. A construction company might hire a marine geologist to locate sand and gravel aggregates for use in building roads. The tidal motions or the strength and direction of currents would be of interest to a physicist. Because the oceans greatly impact the climate and weather, meteorologists must study *oceanography*, the science encompassing the physical geography of the oceans and seas, in order to understand atmospheric circulation patterns and predict effects of phenomena such as El Niño.

Naval authorities originally supported oceanic and coastal explorations to gain information useful for military strategy and maneuvers. Economic incentives also motivated nations to explore the deep sea for food, minerals, and oil. As awareness of the scientific implications of the research increased in the 19th century, naturalists began accompanying crews on survey and cargo vessels to learn about the wildlife at the exotic destinations. The laying of the first transatlantic cable for radio transmissions required extensive research about the physical and chemical conditions of the ocean floor. Eventually researchers had the technology to explore the oceans and were able to convince others (who could provide financial support for such expeditions) of the worth in learning more about the oceans and their contents. Unexpected discoveries in marine science have advanced knowledge in other areas, including evolution and biotechnology.

Scottish naturalist Sir C. Wyville Thomson directed the first purely scientific oceanographic expedition aboard the HMS *Challenger* from 1872–76. His crew systematically collected massive amounts of biological, chemical, and geological data from the world's oceans and discovered thousands of new species, giving rise to oceanography as a new field of science. The only ocean unexplored by the *Challenger* was the Arctic Ocean, a challenge that Norwegian explorer Fridtjof Nansen bravely tackled. Famous for trekking across the Greenland icecap in 1888 and for reaching the farthest point north in 1895, Nansen's arctic voyages accumulated information that was invaluable to biologists, oceanographers, and meteorologists. Methods for studying the depths of the oceans were limited to unsophisticated techniques such as dredging and trawling, but man yearned to venture into the mysterious depths for direct observation. In the early 1930s, American zoologist William Beebe was one of the first scientists to watch the unique marine life-forms in their own environment by dangling from a ship in a hollow steel bathysphere. As more information about the sea became available, in a movement led by Henry Bigelow, marine scientists began to recognize the need for comprehensive physical, biological, and chemical analysis in understanding the oceans and maintaining their health. During the first half of the 20th century, American zoologist Ernest Everett Just performed pioneering research in the field of embryology, utilizing marine invertebrate organisms as models. Marine geologist Harry Hammond Hess proposed seafloor spreading as the mechanism responsible for creating the oceans; today, his idea is an integral component of the theory of plate tectonics.

Technological advances opened up new possibilities for undersea exploration. Frenchman Jacques-Yves Cousteau invented an underwater breathing device (scuba) that allowed divers to move about freely, and he popularized marine biology by improving underwater photography, bringing vivid imagery of underwater scenery into people's homes. Publicity given to underwater exploration by explorers such as Cousteau and Beebe piqued the interest of countless others, inspiring many to join the ranks of marine scientists. The wonders of the ocean abyss inspired Eugenie Clark to become a world-renowned ichthyologist and the first to study the behavior of sharks. Also interested in marine science from an early age, Sylvia Earle has used scuba as an integral part of her research program to study algae, aquatic ecology, whales, and even underwater habitation by humans. She has increased societal awareness of the need to preserve the oceans and its shores through her jobs, writing, and media involvement. Continued advancements in deep-sea exploration technology enabled Robert Ballard to discover oases of life on the otherwise barren ocean floor and to investigate the geology of mid-oceanic ridges, research that has contributed to the understanding of the evolution of the Earth and its inhabitants.

From advances in comprehending geological processes to the identification of astounding life-forms, these remarkable pioneers of marine science have contributed to the understanding of our blue planet, its history, and its amazing secrets hidden in the deep sea. The nature of the marine sciences makes performing research and collecting data inherently complicated and sometimes dangerous, but these researchers all have been mesmerized by the mysteries of the sea. In order to expand knowledge of the oceans and its inhabitants, they have tenaciously endured and even risked their own safety, each earning for themselves the title of "Pioneer in Science."

Sir C. Wyville Thomson

1

(1830–1882)

Sir C. Wyville Thomson proved that life existed in the depths of the ocean. (*Science Photo Library/ Photo Researchers, Inc.*)

Director of the First Purely Scientific Oceanographic Expedition

In the mid-19th century, not much was known concerning the deep ocean. Although shallow waters had been explored and animal life along the coasts had been surveyed, practically nothing was known of the deep oceans that cover 70 percent of the Earth's surface. How deep were they? What was to be found in the seemingly bottomless abyss? Was there life down there? How did the waters move? A

1

Scottish *naturalist* had the motivation and determination to begin collecting the wealth of information that would form the fabric of a new scientific field. C. Wyville Thomson was scientific director on the world's first scientific oceanographic expedition on the HMS (her majesty's ship) *Challenger*. He debunked the *azoic* theory, which stated that no life existed in the deep ocean. Under his direction, thousands of new species of marine life were discovered, and a vast amount of oceanographic data was amassed, enough to birth the field of oceanography, the scientific study of the sea and all aspects of its contents (physical, chemical, and biological).

A Series of Academic Posts

Charles Wyville Thomson was born to Andrew Thomson, a surgeon, in Bonsyde, Linlithgow, Scotland, on March 5, 1830. As a child he attended Merchiston Castle School. He enrolled in medical school when he was only 16 years old and served as secretary for the Royal Physical Society, which was really more of a natural history society. After three years he had to quit medical school due to health problems. He married Jane Ramage Dawson in 1853, and they had one son, Frank Wyville Thomson, who became a surgeon like his grandfather.

Thomson held a series of academic posts. He was first hired as a *botany* lecturer at the University of Aberdeen in Scotland (1851) but left to serve as professor of natural history at Queen's College in Cork, Ireland (1853). The following year he moved to Belfast to become professor of geology at Queen's College. At Belfast he became well-known as an invertebrate marine biologist, and in 1860 he was named professor of *zoology* and botany. In 1865 he published a landmark paper in the *Philosophical Transactions of the Royal Society* titled "On the Embryogeny of *Antedon rosaceus*." In 1868 he moved once again, accepting a position as professor of botany at the Royal College of Science in Dublin. Finally, in 1870 he landed at the University of Edinburgh, where he was a regius professor of natural history. As a teacher, Thomson was popular. He lectured enthusiastically without notes and always brought props to share with his curious students.

Life in the Azoic Zone

In the mid-1800s, people were curious about the deep ocean for many reasons. At the time, practically nothing was known about them. In the 1850s and 1860s, companies were trying to lay telegraph cable across the ocean. As telegraphy companies improved their technology and expanded, they needed information about the ocean floor, especially concerning its depth and composition. Biologists were interested for the sake of knowledge itself. Knowing that the deep ocean bottom was cold, dark, and under extreme pressure, Scottish naturalist Edward Forbes declared that the ocean had an azoic zone—believing no life existed below a depth of 300 *fathoms*. (One fathom is approximately six feet or 1.8 m.) On a trip to Christiania (present-day Oslo) in 1866, Thomson was inspired by animals he was shown that were supposedly brought up from depths below 300 fathoms. Was there life deep down? If so, where did they get their food? What sorts of adaptations were necessary to support life in what seemed like such an inhospitable environment? Those interested in evolutionary theory wondered if living fossils were to be found hidden under the sea.

Thomson wanted to look for life in the azoic zone and garnered the support of another interested individual, Professor William Benjamin Carpenter from the University of London. Carpenter was the vice president of the Royal Society of London, a highly regarded premier academic organization. Together the men asked the Royal Society for help convincing the Admiralty (the governmental department in charge of the British navy) to give them support for a deep-sea *dredging* expedition. The Admiralty donated the use of a paddle steamer, the HMS *Lightning*. In 1868 Thomson and Carpenter were successful in obtaining specimens of marine life from dredging below 300 fathoms. Dredging is a process for obtaining samples from the bottom of the ocean by use of a framed net or scooping device. They also discovered that the temperature of the deep ocean was not consistently 39.2°F (4°C), as was previously assumed.

With findings that contested two prevailing theories, the men easily were able to obtain further support from the Admiralty for a second expedition. On the HMS *Porcupine*, with John Gwyn

Jeffreys, they performed temperature assays, dredged, and analyzed seawater samples from the west coast of Ireland and off the Shetlands. Amazingly, they obtained evidence of abundant life at 2,435 fathoms. Most of the life-forms belonged to unknown species, and many looked like fossils of animals believed to be extinct.

Following the *Porcupine* cruise, the Royal Society elected Thomson a fellow. He published the results from the *Lightning* and *Porcupine* expeditions in *The Depths of the Sea* in 1873. The findings that life existed down deep and that temperature varied despite similar depths in different regions sparked a renewed general interest in ocean exploration. Thomson took advantage of this by presenting yet another application to the Admiralty and the Royal Society, proposing to systematically study the chemistry, geology, physics, and biology of the oceans. He planned to determine the depths of the sea at hundreds of locations, record temperatures at different levels, chart currents, take bottom mud samples, and most important to Thomson, collect and study the marine life that appeared to exist in the deep ocean.

The Famous *Challenger* Expedition

The proposal was accepted. The British government was not aware that eventually, when the expedition itself and the publishing of all the reports was completed, the bill would exceed £200,000, equivalent today to over $10 million. The Admiralty provided a wooden steam corvette (a small, speedy, lightly armed warship) and crew of approximately 225 men. The ship's captain was George Strong Nares, an experienced survey officer who was later knighted. Within 18 months the HMS *Challenger* was refurbished. Arms were removed, laboratories and civilian quarters were added, and a special platform for dredging was installed. Much storage space was needed for the equipment as well as for the specimens and samples collected.

The *Challenger* expedition departed Portsmouth, England, in December 1872, and would not return for 41 months. It carried Thomson and his staff of five: Scottish chemist John Young Buchanan, English zoologist Henry Nottidge Moseley, Scottish-

Though the HMS *Challenger* had a steam engine, it traveled mostly under sail. *(Courtesy of the National Oceanic and Atmospheric Administration/ Department of Commerce)*

Canadian zoologist and future oceanographer John Murray, German zoologist Rudolf von Willimöes-Suhm, and Swiss artist Jean Jacques Wild. By the time the corvette returned to Spithead in May of 1876, it had traveled over 68,890 nautical miles (as the crow flies), and information from 362 stations had been gathered. The crew performed 492 deep *soundings* and 133 dredgings and sent crates of samples back to Edinburgh from locations such as Bermuda, Halifax, The Cape, Sydney, Hong Kong, and Japan. In all, the *Challenger* crew collected 563 total cases containing 2,270 large glass bottles, 1,794 smaller glass bottles, 1,860 glass tubes, and 176 tin cases of marine specimens preserved in wine spirits. In addition, they had 180 tin cases with dried specimens and 22 casks with specimens in salt water. Amazingly, only four bottles were reported broken, and none of the samples rotted. For this tremendous effort, 10 men gave up their lives.

Every two or three days the *Challenger* would halt at a new station. A bounty of data was gathered at each stop. The naval staff

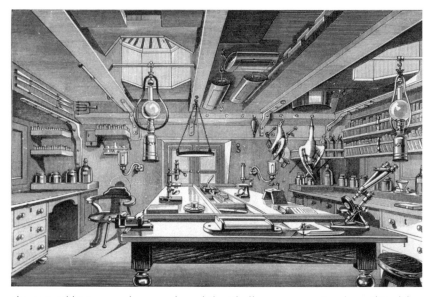

The natural history work room aboard the *Challenger* was uniquely outfitted for collection, study, and storage of samples and specimens collected during the voyage. *(Courtesy of Steve Nicklas, NOS, NGS, and the National Oceanic and Atmospheric Administration/Department of Commerce)*

recorded magnetic, navigational, and meteorological data in addition to observing and noting the direction and speed of surface currents. Attempts also were made to collect subsurface current information, and sounding was performed to measure the depth of the ocean floor. A weighted line, with a bucket attached, was dropped until it hit bottom, then the rope let out was measured to indicate the depth of the sea. When the sounding apparatus hit bottom, a cup-shaped device attached at the end of it would grab a handful of the sediment from the floor for later analysis. The temperature at the floor was recorded using a registering thermometer, and the surface temperature was also noted. Water samples from different depths at each station were taken for chemical analysis. Dredging was performed to obtain samples of marine life from the ocean depths. *Plankton* nets were used to take samples of marine life from mid-level depths to obtain a vertical distribution of life-forms.

In the beginning, the crew, the scientific staff, and Thomson himself were excited each time a haul was brought to the surface, but the work was extremely tedious. It took over an hour to let down equipment into the deep and several hours to wind the dredge rope back up. Several hauls were lost to sea. Men became tired and bored, and without a vested interest, the physical labor seemed monotonous. Over the course of the three and one-half years, 61 men deserted the expedition while harbored. Though the labor was wearisome, the value of the scientific information gathered from this voyage was due to the consistency in the collection of the vast amounts of data. Virtually all the oceans were

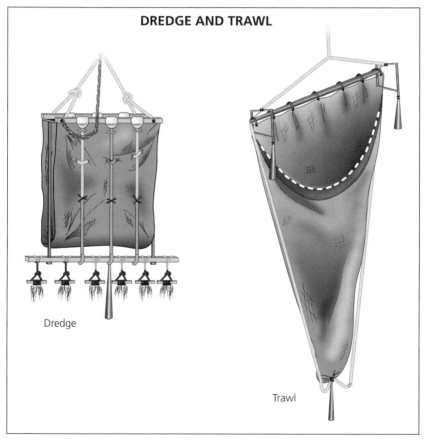

DREDGE AND TRAWL

Dredge

Trawl

Samples were collected using a dredge and a trawl.

explored and analyzed. Comparisons could be made. The reward was astounding.

Remarkably, more than 4,717 new species and 715 new genera were discovered. A countless variety of forms and structures of all invertebrate classes were found at all depths. The deepest dredging was from an astonishing depth of 18,701 feet (5.7 km). The crew performed 25 successful dredgings at depths greater than 14,765 feet (4.5 km). Other information was useful for oceanographers

Mid-Atlantic Ridge

The Mid-Atlantic Ridge is an underwater mountain range that splits the Atlantic Ocean from north to south. Running from Iceland to Antarctica, it is the largest mountain range on Earth. Its discovery led to the theory of *seafloor spreading,* which gave credence to the process of *continental drift* that was suggested by Alfred Wegener. In 1912 the German meteorologist Wegener had proposed that the continents on opposite sides of the Atlantic Ocean were drifting apart. In simple terms, the theory of *plate tectonics* says that the Earth's *crust* is divided into large slabs of solid rock that float over the molten *mantle.*

The Mid-Atlantic Ridge is a prime example of a divergent plate boundary between tectonic plates, where new crust is made as plates pull away from one another. While the cause for the sliding of the plates is not completely understood, it is known that molten magma formed from below rises upward to fill the space created during plate separation. Several fracture zones that run perpendicular to the Mid-Atlantic Ridge and other divergent boundaries are the source of submarine earthquakes.

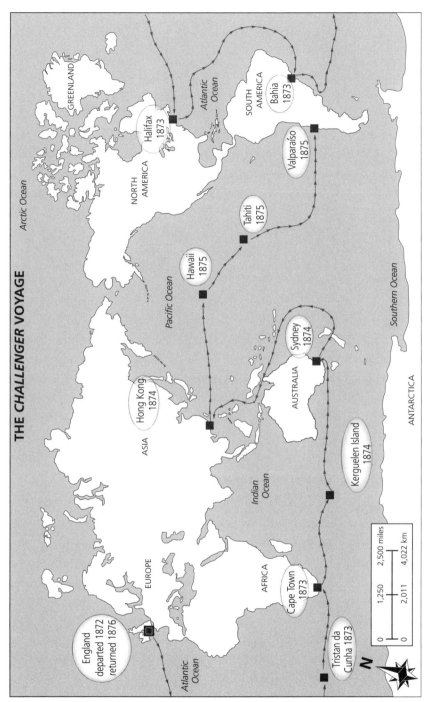

THE CHALLENGER VOYAGE

Arctic Ocean

GREENLAND

NORTH AMERICA

Halifax 1873

Atlantic Ocean

SOUTH AMERICA

Bahia 1873

Valparaíso 1875

Tahiti 1875

Pacific Ocean

Hawaii 1875

Hong Kong 1874

ASIA

Sydney 1874

AUSTRALIA

Kerguelen Island 1874

Southern Ocean

ANTARCTICA

Indian Ocean

EUROPE

AFRICA

Cape Town 1873

England departed 1872 returned 1876

Atlantic Ocean

Tristan da Cunha 1873

| 0 | 1,250 | 2,500 miles |
| 0 | 2,011 | 4,022 km |

N

The *Challenger* expedition traveled 68,890 nautical miles on its three-and-one-half-year voyage.

interested in oceanic circulation. Sediment composition analysis revealed hints of how the ocean floor formed as well as the direction of the subsurface currents. Thomson's staff discovered that a red clay bottom was common at depths below 2,000 fathoms. Above that, they found a distribution of pelagic oozes formed from the calcareous and siliceous shells and spicules from organisms such as foraminiferans and radiolarians.

Sounding data allowed construction of the first contour map of the ocean basins. The deepest sounding was found in the Mariana Trench in the southwest Pacific—a depth of 26,904 feet (8.2 km). They named it the Challenger Deep. One surprising discovery was the existence of a ridge running the length of the ocean, called the Mid-Atlantic Ridge.

In addition to the biological specimens and geological samples, the members of the expedition returned with memories of 568 days spent in the harbors of exotic destinations, including South America, South Africa, Australia, New Zealand, Hong Kong, Japan, and many islands of the Atlantic and the Pacific Oceans. They collected zoological and botanical specimens from these faraway lands as well as their waters. They also learned about other races and the cultures of more primitive societies.

The *Challenger* Reports

After returning from the expedition, Thomson set up an office in Edinburgh. This office was in charge of sorting through the collected materials, distributing them for analysis, and organizing the reporting of the results. Thomson established the format for the *Challenger* reports, but unfortunately his health did not permit him to see this work to completion. He did publish a preliminary account of the voyage, *The voyage of the "Challenger." The Atlantic* (1877), that contained beautiful figures of very ornate life-forms, including echinoderms such as starfish and sponges. Thomson summarized data concerning the contour of the Atlantic bed, the composition of the ocean bottom, the temperature variations, the distribution of deep-sea fauna, the density of sea water, and the amount of carbonic acid contained in sea water. The Pacific complement of this report was never written. In honor of his service to science, Queen Victoria knighted Thomson in 1876. The Royal Society also awarded him a gold medal.

People and institutions fought over the manner in which the samples and specimens were distributed. The British Museum thought they should be in charge of receiving all the samples, organizing their examination, and coordinating the reporting of the results. Some people also felt that the British should be solely in charge of the actual research on the samples and specimens. Thomson believed otherwise. He thought that the research materials should be sent to the most qualified experts for analysis. Over 100 scientists from several nations, including France, Germany, Italy, Belgium, Scandinavia, and the United States, as well as from the United Kingdom, were ultimately involved in the investigations. In addition, the British government was distressed at the total bill. It seemed everyone had something to complain about.

It is likely that all this bickering and stress contributed to the early demise of Thomson at age 52. He suffered a paralytic attack in 1879, then another in 1881, when the original five-year Treasury grant expired. That same year he resigned his professorship at the University of Edinburgh and his directorship of the *Challenger* Commission. Sir C. Wyville Thomson, a man who admired all nature and had extensive knowledge of the natural sciences, died on March 10, 1882, in Bonsyde, Scotland.

One of the junior naturalists from the expedition who later became a famous oceanographer, John Murray, assumed the responsibility of coordinating the completion of all the reports. Though it was originally estimated this task would take about five years and consume 15 volumes, in the end, it took 19 years and filled 50 volumes composed of 29,552 pages. For more than 100 years, oceanographers have relied on the *Report on the Scientific Results of the Voyage of the H.M.S.* Challenger, which is available in countries all over the world. The vast amount of content information as well as the beautiful artwork and photography make it a valuable resource even today. Specimens collected by Thomson's staff are stored at the Natural History Museum in London. The *Challenger* expedition is considered the dawn of the field of oceanography. Geographers, *hydrographers*, and marine biologists are indebted to the man who bore three and one-half years of drudgery and a decade of complaining to open up new fields in marine science.

CHRONOLOGY

1830	Charles Wyville Thomson is born on March 5 in Bonsyde, Linlithgow, Scotland
1846–50	Studies medicine
1851	Is a lecturer in botany at the University of Aberdeen
1853	Is appointed a professor of natural history at Queen's College, Cork
1854	Becomes professor of geology at Queen's College, Belfast
1860	Becomes a professor of zoology and botany at Queen's College, Belfast
1866	Observes animals collected from below 300 fathoms in Christiania, Norway
1868	Accepts a professorship in botany at the Royal College of Science, Dublin, and cruises on the HMS *Lightning*
1869	Cruises on the HMS *Porcupine*
1870	Accepts a regius professorship of natural history at the University of Edinburgh
1872–76	Is the scientific director on the HMS *Challenger* expedition
1873	Publishes *The Depths of the Sea*
1876	Queen Victoria knights Thomson
1877	Publishes *The Voyage of the Challenger: The Atlantic*
1880–95	The *Challenger* reports are published in 50 volumes
1882	Dies on March 10 in Bonsyde, Scotland

FURTHER READING

Challenger Oceanic. "The Voyage of the H.M.S. Challenger (1872–1876)." Available online. URL: http://www.challenger

oceanic.com/chal.htm. Accessed on January 17, 2005. Description and map of the famous expedition.

Gillispie, Charles C., ed. *Dictionary of Scientific Biography.* Vol. 13. New York: Scribner, 1970–76. Good source for facts concerning personal backgrounds and scientific accomplishments but assumes reader has basic knowledge of science.

Linklater, Eric. *The Voyage of the* Challenger. London: John Murray Publishers, 1972. Detailed description of the *Challenger* voyage and the personalities on board. Lots of illustrations.

Rice, A. L. *Voyages of Discovery: Three Centuries of Natural History Exploration.* New York: Clarkson Potter, 1999. Visual record chronicling several significant discoveries in natural science exploration. Beautiful artwork and photographs.

Thomson, C. Wyville. *The depths of the Sea. An account of the general results of the dredging of H.M.S. "Porcupine" and "Lightning" during the summers of 1868, 1869, and 1870, under the scientific direction of Dr. Carpenter, F.R.S., J. Gwyn Jeffreys, F.R.S., and Dr. Wyville Thomson, F.R.S.* London: Macmillan, 1873. Original work by Thomson. Difficult reading but very informational.

———. *The voyage of the "Challenger." The Atlantic; a preliminary account of the general results of the exploring voyage of H.M.S. "Challenger" during the year 1873 and the early part of the year 1876.* London: Macmillan, 1877. Original work by Thomson. Difficult reading but very informational.

Fridtjof Nansen

2

(1861–1930)

Science benefited greatly from Fridtjof Nansen's daring Arctic explorations. (© *The Nobel Foundation*)

Oceanographer and Polar Explorer

In order to make new and amazing discoveries, a scientist must take risks, and Fridtjof Nansen's adventurous spirit led him to father the field of polar exploration. Yet it was his unyielding resolve, brilliance, and willingness to believe in the unpopular that earned him the designation of founder in the fields of neurology as well as oceanography and fluid dynamics (the study of the movements of water). For this he deserves the respect of all successive oceanographers and zoologists. After spending count-less hours looking at the nervous systems of marine invertebrates under a microscope, he dared to challenge the prevailing supposi-tion that the nerves formed a continuous network throughout an organism. His bold declaration and supporting evidence was among the earliest creating the foundation for the modern neuron theory. His ingenuity and extraordinary planning ability allowed him to journey through the unexplored arctic sea and Greenland's interior. During these expeditions, he meticulously gathered immense amounts of information invaluable to biologists, oceanographers, and meteorologists, and he was able to confirm many old assumptions as well as contribute some revolutionary theories of his own.

An Outdoor Childhood

Fridtjof (pronounced Frid-yof) Nansen was born on October 10, 1861, near Christiania, Norway (renamed Oslo). He was the first son born to Baldur Nansen and Adelaide Johanne Thekla Isidore Wedel-Jarlsberg. They already had six children from previous first marriages. The following year they had another son, whom they named Alexander. Fridtjof and Alexander grew up near Nordmarka, a forest, and near a fjord. In the summers they fished and swam, in the fall they hunted with bows and rifles, and in the winters they skied. They often spent days away in the forest sleeping on the ground and eating whatever they killed. Fridtjof was a naturally tal-ented skier. He started skiing at an age when most children learn to speak in sentences. As a young adult he placed in several region-al and national competitions, and he won the Norwegian cross-country skiing championship 12 times. He was more interested in sports than in school, but managed to get through with honors and minimal effort.

A *Viking* Voyage

Fridtjof passed the entrance exam for the University of Christiania (now the University of Oslo) in 1880 but was not set on any certain career path. After considering engineering and forestry, he decided to study zoology (the study of animals). In December of 1881, he passed the exam required to specialize in the study of lower marine creatures. Based on the recommendation of zoology professor Robert Collett, three months later he sailed away on the maiden voyage of a sealing vessel to Spitzbergen (islands off the east coast of Greenland). This four-month trip had a profound influence on Nansen, and thereafter his career was dedicated to the sea.

Nansen's goals on the *Viking* were to learn more about seals and other marine life and to study the ocean's currents. He got along well with the ship's captain, Axel Krefting, but the other crew members were wary of this strange man who spent a lot of time keeping records of temperatures, dissecting seabirds, and peering into his microscope. However, when they reached the ice floes, the habitats of the seals they were hunting, he earned their respect with his bravery and skilled marksmanship. He even talked Krefting into letting him catch a few sharks. When their ship became trapped in the ice on the east side of Greenland, he took to *trawling* for marine life through holes in the ice and hunting polar bears. Nansen admired the icy cliffs ashore, but the captain would not allow him to explore them. One important conclusion Nansen drew from his observations on this trip was that ice forms at the sea's surface, rather than forming underneath and floating to the surface. He also confirmed that water flowed underneath the ice-topped surface. By the end of the voyage, Nansen had achieved the aims for which he set out and had collected many marine specimens, but the sea bug had bit him. He was disappointed to return home.

Studies on the Invertebrate Nervous System

The melancholy did not last. Despite his tender age of 21 and the fact that he had not even completed one year of advanced schooling, he was appointed curator of the Bergen Museum on the west coast of Norway. The museum served as a scientific research institute and thus was an ideal place for Nansen to further his education, since he never appreciated formalized instruction. He threw himself into his work, but he missed skiing, as it did not snow much in Bergen. He missed his hometown so much that he skied home that first Christmas, over the high mountains and through a blizzard!

Nansen continued to work hard, impressing his boss, Dr. Danielssen. Because of the waters surrounding Bergen, he had access to many living marine specimens, which he carefully observed using a new microscope with an oil immersion lens that his father had purchased for him. He labeled and classified many different specimens and had the opportunity to interact with fellow marine scientists. Nansen's interest in the nervous system of marine invertebrates (animals without a backbone) stemmed from a meeting with a German zoologist, Willy Kükenthal. He began teaching himself all there was to be known about specialized nerve cells and the cell theory, which stated that the cell was the basic unit of life and that all organisms were made up of cells. These ideas sprouted throughout the 1800s, as did the theory of evolution. This interested Nansen, because if all living organisms were ancestrally related, then studying the nervous system of lower invertebrates would be useful for understanding human neurophysiology. He specialized in the nervous system of myzostomes, which are parasites of starfish. He was so thorough in his observations and analysis that the Bergen Museum awarded him the Joachim Friele Gold Medal for his first scientific research paper related to these studies.

Yet the man who had spent his youth outdoors was growing restless. In March of 1885, he attempted to resign from the museum, but Danielssen granted him a one-year leave and offered him his salary toward travel expenses. Thus, that summer Nansen visited an *archipelago* north of Bergen that was rich in interesting marine specimens. He wanted to figure out how nerves communicated with each other. The predominant school of thought considered the cells of the nervous system to be continuous, all connected. However, hours upon hours of observation under his microscope convinced Nansen that there were no such direct connections.

The next winter he made his first trip to continental Europe. He visited the renowned cell biologist, Camillo Golgi, in Pavia, to learn a special technique for staining thin tissue sections with silver nitrate. Nansen was the first to use such techniques on the invertebrate nervous system. Though his visit was unannounced, Nansen's charm and eagerness to learn amused Golgi, and he taught him the methodology that would further convince Nansen that nerve cells communicated with each other over open spaces, today termed *synapses*. During his travels, Nansen also charmed his way into being permitted to spend time at a marine biological station in Naples.

Camillo Golgi

Italian Camillo Golgi (July 7, 1843–January 21, 1926) studied medicine at the University of Pavia. After obtaining his medical degree, he worked for seven years at the Hospital of St. Matteo. He became chief medical officer at the Hospital for the Chronically Sick at Abbiategrasso in 1872 and started investigating the nervous system. In 1881 he was appointed the chair of general pathology at the University of Pavia. He never practiced medicine but devoted his life to medical research instead.

His early research included discrimination of three types of parasites that cause malaria and three types of fever. His observations made it possible to diagnose the form of malaria afflicting a patient accurately and to treat the disease more effectively.

Golgi is most famous for inventing a silver staining technique, called the black reaction, that allowed clear microscopic observation of subcellular structures. Based on the perceptive observations on neurons that he was able to make using this technique, he was awarded the Nobel Prize in physiology or medicine in 1906 for his work on the structure of the nervous system. The Nobel was shared with the Spanish anatomist Santiago Ramón y Cajal. The Golgi apparatus, an organelle located in the *cytoplasm* that is responsible for modifying, packaging, and routing substances made in the cell, is named in his honor.

There, and back in Bergen, he applied Golgi's technique and was amazed at the intricacy and detailed images he saw in the stained nervous tissue sections.

Nansen continued his research, making assertions that today are taken for granted. For example, he stated that all nerve units had membranes (it is now known that all cells do). He also observed that nerve fibers branch out into "T" shapes after entering the lower root of the spinal column and was the first to explain theoretically the reflex arc (the path of a simple reflex such as the knee jerk). These structures are the foundation for understanding spinal cord reflexes. The museum published these observations and his historic results that clearly showed there were no unions between nerve cells. Because of the declarations Nansen made in this revolutionary paper, "The Structure and Combination of the Histological Elements of the Central Nervous System," published in *Bergens museums arsberetning* (1886), he is considered one of the founders of modern neurology. Nansen submitted a shortened version of this clearly written English publication in Norwegian as his doctoral dissertation. The university eventually decided to accept the paper as his thesis, and on April 28, 1888, Nansen publicly defended his doctoral dissertation.

Across the Ice Cap

The thoughts consuming his mind, however, were not related to his dissertation; instead they had turned to polar travel. In 1883 explorer Baron Nils Adolf Erik Nordenskiöld returned from an expedition to Greenland's west coast. At the time, the composition of Greenland's interior was unknown. Some thought it might be a balmy paradise, while others, including Nansen, suspected it consisted entirely of ice. He believed he could be the first to venture through Greenland's interior successfully, and he planned to do it on skis. Though most of the world believed Nansen was foolish, one Danish businessman, Augustin Cyrille Victor Vilhelm Gamél, offered to sponsor the expedition. After much careful planning, and after obtaining advice from Nordenskiöld, Nansen led a group of five daring men to the west coast of Greenland by way of a sealing vessel, the *Jason*.

There had been eight previous unsuccessful attempts to break through Greenland's ice cap. All began at the west coast and planned to travel toward the east. Nansen tried the opposite. He figured that if they started on the uninhabited east coast, there would be no retreat location, thus they would be forced to persist along the approximately 430-mile (700-km) proposed route. Nansen estimated this would take approximately one month but packed supplies for two months.

On July 17, 1888, the *Jason* dropped off the explorers within 12.4 miles (20 km) of the east coast. The ship dared not sail any closer due to the choking ice. Within hours the open waters became crowded with potentially crushing ice, so the men were forced to camp out. It took 12 days until they could row ashore and then only to put their boats back in the water a few days later to row up the coast, as they had drifted 236 miles (380 km) south of where the *Jason* left them. They were behind schedule, and Nansen was worried about summer's end as well as a shortage of supplies. He decided to land at Umivik rather than the originally planned Sermilik.

It was August 14 before they started crossing over the huge icy cliffs, lugging the five *sledges* with them. Then, as the climb became less steep, the snow became looser, making skiing more difficult. After being held up for a few more days by rain, they made it over the edge of the ice cap a week later. The conditions varied between smooth traveling and having to cover a surface of sticky snow. Some days they traveled approximately six miles (10 km), others up to 18.6 miles (30 km). One day they covered almost 43 miles (70 km) skiing downhill with the wind behind their backs! Every day, however, all they saw was the same white, flat horizon. Their unvaried and unsatisfying diet became a regular source of complaint among the men, and they were constantly thirsty. Another obstacle was the bitter cold; the temperatures hovered around −58°F (−50°C). In late September, 41 days after they embarked, they traversed the final slope of the ice cap. Nansen had confirmed that Greenland is covered completely by ice. Now the party had soil rather than ice underfoot, but they were still 62 miles (100 km) from their destination of Godthåb.

Nansen and Sverdrup went on ahead. They traveled down a fjord on a makeshift boat and ate gulls they shot along the way. On

October 3, they rowed up to a beach just south of Godthåb, where several Eskimos and one young Danish man, Gustav Bauman, met them. Bauman was thrilled to learn their identities. Amusingly, though the historic first crossing of Greenland had just been accomplished, Bauman offered congratulations to Nansen for earning a doctorate degree, which he had obtained shortly before beginning his expedition. The remainder of the party was fetched, but unfortunately they missed a ship that was departing. Nansen rushed a hastily written summary describing their successful journey to the ship, but the men were forced to live out the winter with the Eskimos. At this time Nansen began considering future polar exploration. The *Hvidbjørnen* arrived in April, bringing a mound of mail for Nansen. In May of 1889, Nansen finally returned to Christiania, where approximately 50,000 people turned out to welcome him.

Danielssen wanted Nansen back at Bergen, but Nansen politely declined. He accepted the post of curator of the zoological collection at the University of Christiania, with the understanding that the post was merely a title and that he would be able to devote his time to writing about his experience. Over the next several months he was invited to give lectures to many different audiences, including the very prestigious Royal Geographical Society in London and the Royal Scottish Geographical Society in Edinburgh. Though he gathered much scientific information during his expedition, especially concerning the meteorological observations that helped explain weather patterns in northern Europe, Nansen portrayed his experience more as a ski tour.

Before Nansen left for Greenland, he had met Eva Sars, the daughter of well-known zoologist Michael Sars, and a famed singer in her own right. Eva was also a talented skier. In August the two became engaged, and though Nansen confessed to her that he planned to make a trip to the North Pole, they were married on September 6, 1889. At first they lived in a primitive, uncomfortable shack at Lysaker. They could not afford much better until Nansen's book *On Skis Across Greenland* was published the following year. The young couple moved into a newly built house they named *Godthåb* (which means "good hope") in the spring of 1891.

Forward!

Nansen believed in the existence of a current that flowed from Siberia through the Arctic Ocean toward Greenland. Pieces of wood collected from his *Viking* voyage and his Greenland expedition that he had analyzed provided evidence in support of this. In addition, a newspaper article from November of 1884 that he had read reported that relics from the wrecked *Jeannette* expedition were found on an ice floe near southwest Greenland. The *Jeannette* had been crushed by ice near the New Siberian Islands. Nansen became committed to making a journey to the North Pole following the predicted current.

Now a national hero, he was easily able to obtain funding from the Norwegian government for his voyage. In February of 1890, he proposed to exploit nature rather than fight it by intentionally allowing his ship to become frozen in the ice and be delivered by the ocean current from Siberia to the North Pole. Thus, the success of this journey depended not only on the actual existence of the proposed current, but also on a specially built ship that was very strong, yet very flexible. Many naval architects thought it impossible to build such a ship, but one brave shipbuilder named Colin Archer took on this challenge. On October 26, 1892, Eva christened the *Fram* (meaning "forward").

Nansen had been incredibly busy, meticulously planning every last detail and preparing for every possible emergency. He had special equipment for ice and snow travel built and ordered food supplies and appropriate clothing. The most difficult part of Nansen's preparation was finding the right men from the many who applied to accompany him. One man on whom Nansen knew he could depend was Otto Sverdrup, with whom he had traversed Greenland. He wanted educated men, other scientists even, but they had to be excellent skiers and have knowledge of the sea and ships. He eventually settled on 12 men.

The *Fram* departed from Oslo Fjord in June of 1893. The voyage was expected to last three years, but they packed for six, just in case. North of the Siberian coast they charted and named several new islands. By September 22, the *Fram* was frozen in the ice. Its design was able to withstand the pressure of the freezing waters. As ice formed, it was lifted above the surface. The ice was not able to grip its rounded bottom, much to Nansen's relief. The direction of travel was now out of the control of the *Fram*'s crew.

Time passed. On October 26, the Sun sank below the horizon not to be seen again for four months. Their sledge dogs had puppies. The men read the 600 books in the ship's library. They worried about scurvy and went for walks on the ice. Sometimes they quarreled; sometimes they doubted their decision to make this voyage. They celebrated holidays and birthdays with cakes. Meanwhile, Nansen's theory about the arctic current was proving to be true. However, travel toward the north was much slower than desired. It did not appear that drifting alone was going to get them close enough. By 1894 Nansen was secretly considering leaving the *Fram* to travel on skis to the pole.

Meteorological and geographical observations were carried out regularly. Nansen examined specimens he dredged up under the microscope. Daily he noted the water's temperature, *salinity*, and the thickness of the ice. Soundings demonstrated that the polar waters were much deeper than previously imagined. Nansen also noticed that the ice did not drift exactly in the direction of the wind but at a 45° angle to it. He suspected this was due to the Earth's rotation and later passed the task of proving this mathematically to Vagn Walfrid Ekman, whose legacy is the Ekman spiral (though one could argue it should be called the Nansen-Ekman spiral). From his observations Nansen also proposed the existence of an underwater ridge near Greenland, now called the Nansen Ridge.

Farthest North

Late in 1894, Nansen informed his men that he planned to leave the *Fram* with one other in hopes of reaching the North Pole. While Sverdrup may have been an excellent companion for such an adventure, he needed to continue captaining the ship. Nansen chose F. Hjalmar Johansen, the ship's stoker. Months were spent preparing special kayaks, reindeer fur sleeping bags, clothing, and food. After two disheartening false starts, Nansen and Johansen left their warm, comfortable, floating home on March 14, 1895, at a latitude

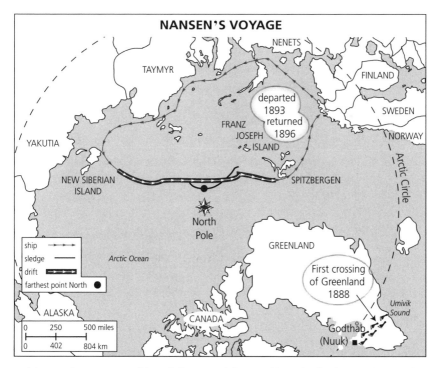

In his travels, Nansen achieved the record for reaching the farthest point north.

of 84°4', already farther north than anyone had previously reached. A team of 28 sledge dogs pulling three sledges loaded high with all their supplies accompanied the two.

They discovered that sledge dogs traveled at about the same rate as men cross-country skiing. They trudged along during the days and pitched a tent and dried their wet clothes by the stove each night. At one point they lost their sledge meter and thus had to rely on astronomical observations to determine their position. As March ended, their latitude readings were much lower than expected. Nansen began to worry that they might not be able to reach the pole as the ice was now drifting south faster than they were traveling north. On April 7, at a latitude of 86°24' N, 146 miles (235 km) farther than the record, Nansen and Johansen ceremonially planted a Norwegian flag into the ice and turned around. They were about 230 miles (370 km) from the pole and about 400 miles (644 km) from their next planned destination, Franz Josef Land.

For the next several months, Nansen and Johansen faced several tribulations, including not knowing their precise location, as both of their watches stopped one day and their positioning calculations depended on knowing the exact time. They had expected to reach land by June but were still wandering about. The dogs were slowly starving, and one by one they were killed off to feed the rest of the pack. Nansen and Johansen killed seals, walruses, and polar bears when they could, feasted off the meat, used the fat for stove fuel, and used the hides for warmth. In August they landed on an unknown island, and the weather trapped them there for the upcoming polar winter.

Using bones, driftwood, moss, and walrus hides, they built a hut on the side of a rocky slope. In this 10 × 6-foot (3 × 1.8-m) shelter, they spent a long, boring eight months. They lived off bear soup, bear steaks, and melted snow and sometimes slept for two days straight. The temperature in the hut hovered around freezing. On May 19, 1896, the two men left their primitive home and alternately kayaked and skied in what they hoped was the correct direction. On June 17, Nansen heard dogs barking and left Johansen to make sure the sledges did not float away as they had once before. Upon investigating Nansen saw fresh tracks. Soon he met up with Englishman Frederick George Jackson, who ironically had applied and been rejected to accompany Nansen on this voyage. Nevertheless, he had been hoping to meet up with Nansen and even had a stack of letters for him. A search party was sent to fetch Johansen, and both men were treated like heroes. They were at Cape Flora, Franz Josef Land. The longhaired, bearded, greasy, sooty, disheveled travelers were treated with hot baths and transformed back into clean, shaven, respectable-looking men. They enjoyed coffee, sugar, and other luxuries while they patiently waited for an expected ship to arrive. Nansen passed time geologizing on the *basalt* cliffs.

The *Windward* arrived on July 26 and departed with its excited passengers on August 7. On August 13, 1896, they approached the Norwegian coast and stopped at Vardø, where Nansen immediately telegraphed Eva and countless others. The good news traveled fast, and the homecoming was a joyous celebration. On August 18, Eva met her husband at Hammerfest, where an incredible reception awaited them. Coincidentally, only two days later Nansen received a telegram from Sverdrup saying the *Fram* had also just arrived back in Norway after its three-year excursion. They met back up in Tromsø, where Nansen, his wife, and Johansen rejoined the *Fram* to return together to Christiania, where the reception was tremendous. No one seemed to care that Nansen had not actually reached the North Pole. He broke the record for farthest north, suffered no loss of life on his journey, and made many scientific discoveries that would spark a new interest in physical oceanography for years to come. He was an international hero. A series of lectures and celebratory banquets ensued. Both Oxford and Cambridge Universities conferred honorary degrees upon him.

Barely two months later, Nansen completed a 300,000-word account of his expedition in Norwegian. The English version came out the next January and included diary passages. Both texts were a huge financial success. His scientific findings concerning the arctic seas were published later (1900–06) in a series of six volumes (*The Norwegian North Polar Expeditions, 1893–1896*) that were as popular among scientists as his less detailed accounts were among the general public.

Oceanographer Recipient of Nobel Peace Prize

Nansen was given a research professorship in zoology at the University of Christiania. He settled somewhat into a family life with his wife and a daughter born just before he left on the *Fram*, and soon had another daughter and three sons. They bought a house overlooking the fjord and named it *Polhøgda*.

Eventually he began researching again. In 1900 he became director of the International Laboratory for North Sea Research at Christiania. Over the next decade Nansen was sought as a lecturer and consultant, and in 1908 he was given the new position of chair of oceanography at Christiania. As Norway's economy was dependent upon fishing, information concerning ocean currents, sea depths, and temperatures as well as fish habitats was invaluable. He developed several pieces of equipment for collecting and analyzing seawater, currents, and marine life. These improvements allowed significant contributions to be made in the new field of oceanography. He also journeyed through Siberia in 1913 to help develop a trade route from Siberia to Europe.

Nansen made his mark as a marine zoologist, became infamous as a polar explorer, and advanced the field of oceanography, but his involvements later in life took him in entirely new directions. He became the first Norwegian delegate to the League of Nations (the seed of today's United Nations). He was responsible for successfully organizing the repatriation of more than 437,000 prisoners from World War I with only minimal finances. In addition, he solicited financial and other support and directed the aid to millions of people starving in Russia as a result of a serious drought-induced famine. This was no easy accomplishment, as many countries were resistant to help the Russians for fear it would be seen as supporting the communists. He next took on the task of arranging travel and finding homes for more than 1.5 million refugees. His contributions led to his being awarded the Nobel Peace Prize in 1922 for his humanitarian efforts.

Fridtjof Nansen died of a heart attack on May 13, 1930, while sitting on a porch chair overlooking the sea. He was given a state funeral on Norway's Independence Day, May 17, and was laid to rest at *Polhøgda* in Lysaker.

Robert Peary was the first to reach the North Pole in 1909, and Roald Amundsen was the first to reach the South Pole in 1911. Both were dreams Nansen had held. Yet his overwhelming achievements in oceanography, marine zoology, and polar exploration carried science further than having simply been the first to do something. The *Fram* has been preserved in its own museum in Oslo, serving as a reminder of the man who loved the process of discovery and was willing to take risks to make advances.

CHRONOLOGY

1861	Fridtjof Nansen is born on October 10 in Store-Fröen, Norway
1882	Goes on *Viking* expedition and becomes curator at the Bergen Museum

1886   Publishes "The Structure and Combination of the Histological Elements of the Central Nervous System," in *Bergens museums arsberetning* and receives the Friele Gold Medal of the Bergen Museum

1887   Visits Germany and Italy

1888   Receives a doctorate degree from the University of Christiania for his dissertation on the central nervous system of certain lower invertebrates

Nansen and five companions are dropped off by the *Jason* near the east coast of Greenland on July 17. They begin the trek across Greenland on August 16. On October 3, Nansen and his team reach the village of Godthåb, on the west coast of Greenland

1889   Nansen returns to Norway and is appointed curator at the University of Christiania.

1893   Sets sail for the North Pole on the *Fram* in June

1895   After leaving the *Fram* to attempt a trek to the North Pole, Nansen and Johansen set a record on April 7 for reaching the farthest point north

1896   Nansen arrives back in Norway and becomes chair of zoology at the University of Christiania

1900   Becomes director of the International Laboratory for North Sea Research at Christiania

1900–06   Publishes *The Norwegian North Polar Expeditions, 1893–1896* in six volumes

1908   Becomes the chair of oceanography at Christiania

1913   Journeys through Siberia

1920   Becomes the first Norwegian delegate to the League of Nations

1922   Receives the Nobel Peace Prize

1930   Dies on May 13 from a heart attack in Oslo

FURTHER READING

Denzel, Justin F. *Adventure North: The Story of Fridtjof Nansen.* London and New York: Abelard-Schumann, 1968. Vividly describes Nansen's expeditions. Appropriate reading for middle school students.

Gillispie, Charles C., ed. *Dictionary of Scientific Biography.* Vol. 15. New York: Scribner, 1970–76. Good source for facts concerning personal backgrounds and scientific accomplishments but assumes reader has basic knowledge of science.

Huntford, Roland. *Nansen: The Explorer as Hero.* London: Gerald Duckworth and Company, 1997. Focuses on *Fram* expedition but honestly explores other aspects of Nansen's life as well.

Nobelprize.org. "The Nobel Peace Prize 1922." Available online. URL: http://nobelprize.org/peace/laureates/1922. Last modified on June 16, 2000. Includes links to Nansen's biography, Nobel speech, a related article, and other resources.

Noel-Baker, Francis. *Fridtjof Nansen: Arctic Explorer.* New York: Putnam, 1958. Account of Nansen's life, adventures, and accomplishments in story format. Appropriate for juvenile readers.

William Beebe

3

(1877–1962)

William Beebe (left), shown here with colleague Otis Barton, explored marine life at great ocean depths in the bathysphere. (© *Wildlife Conservation Society*)

Exploration of Deep-Sea Life

Given the freedom to travel to where no man has gone before and see what no man has ever seen, some brave souls would venture into outer space. Others might imagine themselves far inside a secluded forest, deep in an unknown cave, on a remote island, or perhaps under the sea. William Beebe was one of the first men to venture into the ocean depths. In a hollow steel sphere, he dangled in the mysterious blackness and discovered hundreds of new marine species. He began his scientific career as an ornithologist and became popular as a scientific adventure writer.

Early Interest in Wildlife

Charles William Beebe was born on July 29, 1877, in Brooklyn, New York. His father, Charles Beebe, was a paper dealer, and his mother, Henrietta Marie Youngblood Beebe, was an ambitious woman who was determined to help her son succeed. The Beebes had a second son who died at age 15 months. In early childhood William's family moved to the first of a series of homes in East Orange, New Jersey.

William attended Ashland Grammar School and before entering East Orange High School, he dropped Charles from his name. He completed four years of Latin as well as two years of German, languages that would help him later in his career. In addition, he took several courses in the natural sciences. He was a strong student and very physically active. In his spare time he watched and listened to birds, memorized the local wildflowers, collected butterflies, and built up a bird nest collection. Before he even graduated, he had his first scientific publication, a letter to the editor of *Harper's Young People* about a bird, the brown creeper.

After high school he matriculated as a special student at the University of Columbia. He took many classes there and attended several lecture series, but he never received his degree. Though never a degree candidate, Will did make the acquaintance of people who helped advance his career. One noteworthy man was paleontologist Henry Fairfield Osborn, a professor at Columbia and the curator of the American Museum of Natural History. Osborn was a founder of the New York Zoological Society (NYZS, now the Wildlife Conservation Society), and in 1895 he became its first president. The society opened a Zoological Park (the present-day Bronx Zoo) in 1899.

In October of 1899, Beebe was hired as the zoo's first assistant curator for birds. Beebe claimed this was why he never obtained his baccalaureate degree from the University of Columbia. What Beebe lacked in formal training, he made up for in zest. Several of his articles had already been published in popular magazines, but now they started appearing in scientific publications such as *Science*,

The Auk, and later *Zoologica*. In 1902 he was promoted to curator, and he piloted campaigns to build a spacious large bird house and a humongous flying cage.

Wilderness Adventures

Mary Blair Rice became Beebe's wife in 1902. She traveled with Will and collaborated on many of his writing projects. They traveled to Mexico together during the winter of 1903–04. The goal of the trip was to identify and collect Mexican bird specimens, especially those not indigenous to the southern United States. Though Mary had never ridden before, they traveled on horseback and slept in tents. Mary was well educated and a talented writer in her own right. She assisted in writing Beebe's first published work, *Two Bird Lovers in Mexico* (1905).

Field research dominated Beebe's interests, and writing occupied his time. *The Bird, Its Form and Function* was an introduction to ornithology. It was his first book, though it was actually published in 1906, after two others. He dedicated it to his mentor, Osborn.

Another popular book intended to inspire amateur naturalists was *The Log of the Sun*, written by Beebe and published in 1906. Composed of 52 chapters, one for each week of the year, the book was very poetic and included essays on topics ranging from the life sciences to meteorology. In 1910 Will and Mary Beebe wrote another book together, *Our Search for a Wilderness*, describing two expeditions they took together, one to northeastern Venezuela in 1908 and another to British Guiana (present-day Guyana) in 1909. Beebe observed the exotic wildlife and brought home some birds for the Zoological Park. He captured 40 birds of 14 different species in Venezuela and 280 birds of 51 species in British Guiana. One interesting encounter was the hoatzin, a strange bird whose young have claws on the back of their wings for climbing trees.

Beebe traveled with his wife to eastern Asia from 1909 to 1911 to study over 20 different pheasant genera. They visited 20 countries in over 17 months, but unfortunately, the two did not get along as well back home as they did in the wilderness. In January 1913, Mary left Beebe and bitterly divorced him later that year after 11 years of marriage. Beebe took a privately funded five-year leave to pursue museum research and complete the major scientific publication of his career, *A Monograph of the Pheasants* (1918–22). Only 600 sets of this very expensive four-volume work were printed. The series was as popular among painters for the beautiful photographs and sketches of pheasants as it was among naturalists for the extensive knowledge it contained. General information about each species, its distribution, description, and life history was presented. Unusual for scientific writing, Beebe used the first person singular and very colorful prose. He vividly shared his own personal adventures in searching for the birds.

The first volume of this project was published in 1918, but the war the United States declared on Germany delayed publication of the remaining three volumes. Almost 40 years old, Beebe volunteered for service during the war, though the nature of his service is somewhat unclear. He served through the French Aviation Service rather than the United States'. While enlisted, he learned to fly and instructed other volunteers. After one year, he returned to the United States, but tastes of his wartime experiences peppered his future writings.

In 1926 and 1927, less scientific, abridged versions of the four-volume *Monograph* were published. These editions, titled *Pheasant Jungles* and *Pheasants, Their Lives and Homes*, were aimed at a more general audience. The latter contained entertaining yet educational fictionalized accounts of his actual experiences. Some scientists scoffed at Beebe's popular writings, claiming it detracted from his reputation as a respectable scientist. In fact, they accused him of exaggerating many of the adventurous claims he recorded in his popular texts. Beebe did not seem too bothered by this. He continued to publish objective scientific accounts of his field research as well as write successful, creative books for the general population.

After returning from his five-year pheasant sabbatical in 1915, Beebe traveled to Brazil to collect bird specimens for the thriving Zoological Park. While there, he was amazed at the number and variety of organisms located within a small region underneath one huge cinnamon tree. He pioneered the method of studying one small designated location for an extended period of time. Significantly, he discovered 76 different types of birds and over 500 total organisms within a few square feet. Beebe's interests switched from birds to tropical research.

Tropical Research

In 1916 Beebe established the NYZS's first tropical research station at Kalacoon, near Georgetown in British Guiana, in the northeastern region of South America. The staff shared their quarters with

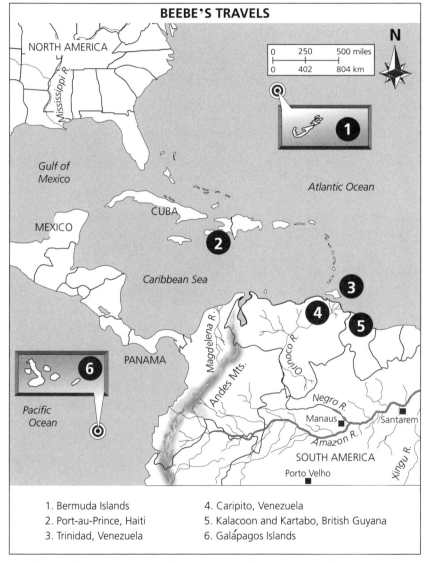

BEEBE'S TRAVELS

1. Bermuda Islands
2. Port-au-Prince, Haiti
3. Trinidad, Venezuela
4. Caripito, Venezuela
5. Kalacoon and Kartabo, British Guyana
6. Galápagos Islands

As director of tropical research for the New York Zoological Society, Beebe traveled extensively to identify species and collect specimens.

scorpions, tarantulas, and vampire bats. Beebe found and studied 281 bird species while at Kalacoon. The Zoological Society published much of his findings and those of two other scientists from this research station in *Tropical Wildlife in British Guiana* in 1917. This book included observations on the bright-billed toucans, the reptilelike hoatzins, and the ground-dwelling tinamous. Beebe added to this account in *Jungle Peace* (1918), for which the former president Theodore Roosevelt wrote the introduction.

After returning from his war service, Beebe was given the title of honorary curator of the department of birds. In addition, the society created a department of tropical research that Beebe directed from 1922 until he retired. When his staff returned to Kalacoon, the *ecology* of the region had changed due to the number of rubber trees that had been cut down for war supplies. They moved the research station to nearby Kartabo, at the junction of the Cuyuni and Mazaruni Rivers. Beebe wrote several scientific papers describing the flora and fauna of the jungle there. *Edge of the Jungle* (1921) and *Jungle Days* (1925) were both inspired by Kartabo. They focused on the ecology of jungle life. Beebe's professional interests were expanding once again. A 1926 issue of *Zoologica* included a paper he wrote on the three-toed sloth.

In the spring of 1923, Beebe journeyed to the Galápagos Islands. He spent two and one-half months at sea on the *Noma* but only 100 hours on the islands themselves. Island mockingbirds delighted him by running up to welcome him rather than flying. The tameness of all the wildlife there enamored the naturalist. Immersed in birds, sea lions, and iguanas, he pondered the irregular variations between the island species. The expedition spent some time anchored in Darwin Bay, which they named, where they were surprised to find bits of coral on the beach. Beebe was harmlessly attacked there by a two-foot (61-cm) moray eel, and they took pleasure in watching birds fight over prime nest-building sticks.

The *Arcturus* Expedition

Soon after returning to New York with plant and animal specimens gathered for the Zoological Park and the American Museum of Natural History, Beebe ventured out again, this time on a steam yacht called *Arcturus*. His main focus now was oceanography, in particular, creatures of the sea. He also planned to study the Sargasso Sea south and east of Bermuda and the Humboldt Current, which moves up the Pacific coast of South America toward the Galápagos.

The *Arcturus* departed Brooklyn in February of 1925 for a six-month trip. Unfortunately, storms stirred up the Sargasso Sea too much for study to be useful and the Humboldt Current was unexpectedly absent. Nevertheless, much valuable information was collected. After five weeks out, the ship needed some repairs, so they rested at Fort Sherman, Panama, for a while. Beebe took pleasure in examining the wildlife there.

Next they anchored at their previous lodging, Darwin Bay, and continued exploring and collecting. It was here that Beebe began to use a copper diving helmet as an integral part of his field research. The helmet allowed him to remain submerged for long periods of time. A leather tube ran from the helmet to a vessel above the surface, and a person hand-pumped fresh air down the tube to the diver. Using a helmet, he was able to collect specimens that had never before been identified and to view marine life in the natural environment. Animals were brought above the surface for further live study in his aquariums or by dissection.

While they were stationed at Darwin Bay, the crew happened to observe volcanic fires from Albemarle, the largest island of the Galápagos archipelago. They set out in that direction. When Beebe crazily decided to explore up close with his foremost assistant John Tee-Van, the gas and smoke made them nauseous, and Beebe temporarily lost some sight and speech. After stumbling back to the ship, he was severely dehydrated and exhausted, but he recovered. When passing by again nine weeks later, they were amazed to witness the red-hot lava flowing into the ocean waters. The hot waters killed many fish that swam too close. Scavengers became ill from unknowingly approaching the gaseous exhalations and died as well. The crew watched one sea lion tragically jump high out of the hot water right into the lava.

When Beebe left the Galápagos in June of 1925, he had plenty of research material. As usual, he shared highlights of his experiences as well as scientific information through his writing. *Galápagos:*

World's End and *The* Arcturus *Adventure* were published in 1924 and 1926, respectively. At the time, there was still much debate over the origin of the islands. Some believed, as scientists do today, that the archipelago was formed from a volcanic hotspot that spewed out hot magma that piled up over time to form the individual islands. In *Galápagos: World's End*, Beebe stated his belief that the islands were originally one continuous landmass that sunk, leaving portions above the sea surface, thus creating the archipelago. This would explain the similarities between species on the islands, yet allow for evolution of unique characteristics by adaptation over time. Beebe also believed that a landbridge formerly existed connecting the Galápagos Islands to the Cocos Ridge. This would explain how terrestrial animals and insects and spiders originally arrived on the islands. Others who believed in the idea of a former landbridge thought it probably connected with Ecuador, which would have been closer. Beebe always remained open-minded if proof otherwise was presented. As it turns out, two years later on the *Arcturus* expedition, Beebe himself ended up making observations that led him to believe that terrestrial creatures could have come to inhabit the islands in the absence of a landbridge. In *The* Arcturus *Adventure* (1981) Beebe imaginatively described the eruption of Albemarle.

> I watched an open artery of Mother Earth pouring into the sea—rock liquid as blood. The Galápagos were being born again. (137)

During his *Arcturus* expedition, Beebe set up a sea station halfway between the Galápagos Islands and Central America, 60 miles (97 km) south of Cocos Island. A sea station was a designated area where the boat remained stationary or slowly circled, while the staff hauled up nets, dredged, took bottom samples, recorded temperatures, and made other observations. At one of these temporary data-gathering locations, named number 74, a remarkable 136 fish species and over 50 crustacean species were captured in a 10-day period. This was quite long to stay in one spot, but they were having too much success to leave. In this location, Beebe took surface hauls every 30 minutes for an entire day. This allowed him to observe that some fish only surfaced during the daytime, while others surfaced only at night. This was useful information for marine biologists so that if they wanted to study a particular type of fish, they knew when they were most likely to find it. He also figured out that data on *luminescent* fish was best gathered at nighttime, and he was able to make rare observations of living luminescent fish.

Haiti and Bermuda

By July the expedition had returned to New York, leaving Beebe to sort through his data and numerous specimens. It was obvious that now he was hooked on marine biology. The following year, he set out for Haiti on a schooner chartered by the NYZS. A biological station was set up on board the *Lieutenant* in the Bay of Port-au-Prince, where they stayed for four months. The goal was to identify fish in Haitian waters and explore the coral reefs. From this expedition he wrote *Beneath Tropic Seas* (1928). A list of 270 species was published in *Zoologica* in 1928 and grew to 324 species when the list was supplemented in 1934. Thus the first goal was achieved. To study coral reef life, Beebe depended on his diving helmet. In over 300 dives, Beebe observed diverse life-forms of the coral reef and then classified them by their ecological niche.

While in Haiti, Beebe met Elswyth Thane, a writer for newspapers and motion picture studios. They married in 1927. Will dedicated *Beneath Tropic Seas* to his young wife. They traveled together and separately, both of them involved in their own research.

In 1928 Beebe obtained permission from the British government to carry out studies on the island of Nonsuch in Bermuda. The region of focus was eight miles (13 km) in diameter and ranged from 6,000 to 8,000 feet (1,829 to 2,438 km) deep. Most of Beebe's research over the next 11 years was carried out here, including his most famous deep-sea dives. Of course, the goal was to study fish from the deep sea as well as from the shores. Beebe and Tee-Van published *Field Book of the Shore Fishes of Bermuda* (1933). They used many of the common research methods that had been used for decades, including trawling, dredging, and hauling silk nets, but Beebe found these means limiting.

Beebe had been the first to use a diving helmet as an integral part of his field research rather than just for pleasure, but its utility was limited. It was fine for dives between 15 and 50 feet (4.6–15.2 m) deep, but by 100 feet (30.5 m) it became unsafe. Humans had pre-viously survived dives of 150 feet (45.7 m) deep for about three min-utes. Submarines descended to approximately 350 feet (107 m), and the record for a diver in a rigid metal suit was 525 feet (160 m). Beebe contemplated alternative means of underwater exploration.

The Bathysphere Dives

Meanwhile, a 1926 newspaper article had announced Beebe's plans to pursue the design of a cylindrical-shaped *submersible* for direct observation of underwater life. This caught the attention of a young man named Otis Barton. Barton was trained in engineering at Harvard University and was in the midst of postgraduate work in natural history at Columbia University. He had his own plans to explore the ocean in a specially designed underwater vessel. Following the news article in 1926, Beebe received numerous let-ters from people who wanted to join him in his efforts. Most of the submitted plans were underdeveloped or from underqualified indi-viduals, leaving Beebe to ignore the bulk of his mail. Several attempts by Barton at reaching Beebe were fruitless. They finally met in December 1928, and Barton presented blueprints for a spherical vessel. In addition to the ingenious design, Barton said he was willing to finance the construction of the *bathysphere* from his late grandfather's inheritance. Beebe was immediately impressed, and the project commenced.

One major feat of the vessel design was to withstand the enor-mous pressure from the ocean depths. Every 33 feet (10 m) of water they descended translated into an additional 14.6 pounds (6.6 kg) per square inch of pressure. Thus at a depth of 3,000 feet (914 m), the hollow ball would have to bear over 7,000 tons of pressure. As odd as it looked, the proposed round bathysphere was actually well suited to evenly distribute the external pressure. Each window would be pressed upon by 19 tons of water. If a mistake was made, the submerged men could be crushed to death in a frac-tion of a second.

The first vessel constructed weighed five tons, too heavy for the barge that would have to carry it out to the ocean. After melting and recasting it, the second attempt was a more acceptable 5,000 pounds. The outer diameter of the newly named "bathysphere" was four feet nine inches (145 cm), and the walls were one and one-half inches (3.8 cm) thick. The circular door was a mere 14 inches (36 cm) in diameter, barely enough for a grown man to wedge himself through. The door was fastened by 10 bolts. There were three window ports, two of which were filled with eight-inch (20-cm) fused

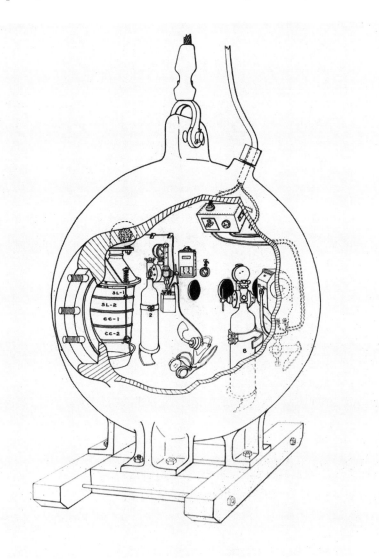

The bathysphere was specially outfitted for deep, underwater exploration of marine life. (© *Wildlife Conservation Society*)

quartz discs, three inches (7.6 cm) thick. The third was plugged. There were four legs on the bottom to which wooden skids were attached. Inside were pans of calcium chloride to absorb moisture and soda lime for absorbing excess carbon dioxide. Of course, oxygen tanks supplied air for breathing. To circulate air inside the chamber, the two men carried palm-leaf fans. An electrical line and a communications line were wrapped together in a cable one and one-half inches (3.8 cm) thick and fed into the top of the sphere. The 3,500 feet (1,067 m) of steel cable necessary to lower the bathysphere into the water weighed 4,000 pounds (1,814 kg). Two steam winches on deck moved the enormous hollow ball.

Unmanned test descents commenced in early June of 1930. The first test resulted in a tangled mess of communication lines. After adjustments and another unmanned descent, the first manned descent occurred on June 6. Despite a minor leak and a pop from an electric switch at around 300 feet (91 m), Beebe and Barton achieved a depth of 800 feet (244 m). Beebe's most amazing observation concerned the colors viewed below the surface. Whereas the water near the surface was a light greenish color, as they descended it turned bluish green, pale blue, then a blackish blue. On June 10, Beebe and Barton made another attempt, but at 250 feet (76 m) the communications line failed. Without being able to hear the human voice from the surface through Beebe's headphones, the men felt very isolated. The crew pulled them up immediately.

After cutting off 300 feet (91 m) of cable, they went down again the following day. They descended slowly, making verbal observations every foot of the way. Beebe's experience in *ichthyologic* identification qualified him for this task. He was thrilled to observe several specimens that previously had only been seen dead in net hauls. Many were brand new, and Beebe and Barton relished the opportunity to observe them swimming in their natural environment. At 1,426 feet (435 m), they paused and returned to the surface. Barton donated the bathysphere to the NYZS that fall.

Two years later history was made again, but this time the world was invited along. The National Broadcasting Company arranged a live broadcast of a dive one Sunday afternoon in September of 1932. The weather had caused delays, and the sea was still rougher than would normally be acceptable, but the world was waiting. Beebe and Barton descended on their 20th deep dive into the sea, and their eager reports to Gloria Hollister aboard the barge were relayed to America. The British Broadcasting Corporation was also connected by short wave radio, increasing the size of the listening audience.

In the bathysphere all light had disappeared by 1,700 feet (518 m), but as they continued descending, the numbers of luminescent fish increased. They turned around after dangling momentarily at 2,200 feet (671 m), and on the way back up Beebe spotted two six-foot (1.8-m) long fish that he named *Bathysphaera intacta* (untouchable bathysphere fish). He claimed their teeth were luminous, and a linear formation of lights decorated their sides. Others later doubted Beebe really saw these, believing perhaps they were a few fish swimming end to end. On this trip, a spiny lobster had been tied to the outside of the bathysphere. The crustacean was expected to be crushed and act as bait to attract fish to the submerged bathysphere for observation, but astonishingly, the lobster survived the thousands of tons of pressure and went on to live in Beebe's aquarium.

The following year, the bathysphere was displayed at the Century of Progress Exposition in Chicago. The president of the National Geographic Society (NGS) asked Beebe to consider one more bathysphere expedition. The NGS would sponsor it, and they did not stipulate an attempt at a new depth record. This sounded attractive to Beebe, who later stated that it was the lack of a request for a new record that made him determined to set one.

The new record dive occurred on August 15, 1934. They reached 3,028 feet (923 m), over one-half mile deep. This record was unbeaten for 15 years. Actually, Beebe and Barton had descended to 2,510 feet (765 m) a few days prior, but Beebe felt that the second dive was totally different despite the exact same location. Several new species were named. Again, Beebe noted the increased number of luminescent fish in deeper regions, and that larger creatures were more prevalent.

The following passage from "A Descent into Perpetual Night" from *Half Mile Down* (1934) helps convey Beebe's appreciation for deep-sea life. They had begun their ascent after an exciting and tense voyage.

. . . but I was slumped down, relaxed. Suddenly I leaned forward, banging my head against the steel but not losing a second of observation. A small school of luminous fish had just passed, when, fortunately at a moment of suspension, came a new and gorgeous creature. I yelled for continuance of the stop, which was at 1900 feet, and began to absorb what I saw; a fish almost round, with long moderately high, continuous, vertical fins; a big eye, medium mouth, and small pectoral fins. The skin was decidedly brownish. We swung around a few degrees to port, bringing the fish into the dark blue penumbra of the beam, and then I saw its real beauty. Along the sides of the body were five unbelievably beautiful lines of light, one equatorial, with two curved ones above and two below. Each line was composed of a series of, pale yellow lights, and every one of these was surrounded by a semicircle of very small but intensely purple photophores.

The fish turned slowly and, head on, showed a narrow profile . . . In my memory it will live throughout the rest of my life as one of the loveliest things I have ever seen. (211-212)

This passage, also from *Half Mile Down*, expresses the amazement Beebe felt when experiencing the true darkness of the deep.

A few days ago the water had appeared blacker at 2500 feet than could be imagined, yet now to this same imagination it seemed to show as blacker than black. It seemed as if all future nights in the upper world must be considered only relative degrees of twilight. I could never again use the word BLACK with any conviction. (221)

The bathysphere experiences were invaluable not only because they set records and revealed undiscovered species, but also because they challenged oceanographers to develop better methods for undersea studies. Beebe emphasized that what was viewed directly was so much different than what was inferred from deep trawling or dredging or net hauls. Observing marine life in the natural environment was much more informative. Many brand-new species were identified and others seen live for the first time. Organisms such as siphonophores (including the Portuguese man-of-war) could be viewed in their true form, rather than as a tangled-up mess of debris brought to the surface. Information on vertical distribution and relative abundance of different species of fish could also be obtained.

After this season, the bathysphere was retired. It was expensive to use and had its limitations. Just like a diving helmet, the sphere had to remain tethered to a surface vessel. Though it had descended over 3,000 feet (914 m), its depths were still limited, as was its

The Bathyscaph

At the World's Fair in Chicago in 1933, a hydrogen-filled balloon was displayed next to the bathysphere. The year before, Swiss physicist Auguste Piccard (1884–1962) had ascended to a record-breaking 53,139 feet (about 10 miles or 16 kilometers) in a pressurized gondola suspended from the balloon. After traveling to dizzying heights to collect data on atmospheric electricity and radioactivity and cosmic radiation, Piccard shifted his focus to the depths of the sea. He designed a submersible called a *bathyscaph,* consisting of two parts, an airtight pressurized cabin and a heptane-filled float for maintaining buoyancy. When the first unmanned test gave disappointing results, Piccard's son Jacques (1922–   ) left his teaching career to lend his assistance to the project. In 1953 the two descended 10,335 feet (about two miles or 3.2 kilometers) into the Mediterranean Sea in the bathyscaph named the *Trieste.* This was over three times the record set in 1934 by Beebe and Barton. In 1958 the U.S. Navy bought the *Trieste,* and Jacques piloted it to a record 35,802 feet (nearing seven miles or 11 kilometers) in the Mariana Trench in the Pacific Ocean in 1960. The Piccards also conceived the idea of the mesoscaphe, a vessel intended for exploring mid-level depths.

lateral mobility. Beebe continued studying oceanography on a yacht named *Zaca*. He continued to use his diving helmet and was as zestful and enthusiastic at the age of 60 as he was at 25 years old. His last sea voyage departed in April 1938.

During World War II, Beebe was unable to continue his research near Bermuda, so he returned to jungle research at Caripito, Venezuela. Beebe's last sea book, *Book of Bays*, was published in 1942. In it, he expressed concern over man's threat to the world's ecosystems. In 1945 he established another research station at Rancho Grande in Venezuela, then yet another that he called Simla, in 1950 in the Arima Valley of Trinidad. He personally purchased this land and lived there during the wintertime. He retired in 1952 and eventually sold this land and its 200 associated acres to the NYZS for one dollar. In 1955 Beebe made one last trip to Asia to check on the pheasant populations he had studied 45 years before.

Inspiration to Others

Though Beebe's spirit remained robust, his health failed during the last three years of his life. He was no longer able to ride his bike around the Zoological Park commanding visitors to go check out the new bird exhibit as he did in his younger days. Unable to tolerate the cold of New York, he spent the months of October through May at Simla. He grew physically weaker and his speech sporadically slurred. Though he expressed hopes of dying of heart failure from viewing an unexpected amazing natural phenomenon, Will Beebe died of pneumonia on June 4, 1962. He was buried in Trinidad.

Simla was renamed the William Beebe Tropical Research Station, but it was functional for only a few more years. The football field–sized bird house at the Zoological Park was replaced by a newer complex in 1972. The bathysphere is on display at the New York Aquarium, which is managed by the Wildlife Conservation Society. During his lifetime, Beebe was criticized for making up fantastical, outlandish tales of extravagant undersea creatures. Years passed before others were able to verify his claims by advancements in underwater photography. Vindicated, he was ultimately recognized for discovering hundreds of new species.

Beebe's scientific articles and notes are recorded in scores of the *Zoological Society's Bulletin* issues and other scientific journals. His two-dozen popular books of naturalist adventures are forever in the hearts of his readers. Some of his readers, such as Rachel Carson and Sylvia Earle, were inspired to embark on their own marine adventures. In the 1950s, underwater breathing machinery, the *aqualung*, and more independent, free-moving underwater vessels were invented. These developments made Beebe's diving helmet and the bathysphere seem ancient, but they had served their purpose. They had opened the way for underwater exploration and inspired a whole new wave of scientists to explore where no human had gone before.

CHRONOLOGY

1877	William Beebe is born on July 29 in Brooklyn, New York
1896–99	Attends the University of Columbia
1899	Becomes assistant curator of birds at the Zoological Park (now the Bronx Zoo)
1902	Becomes curator of birds at the Zoological Park
1905	Publishes first book, *Two Bird Lovers in Mexico*
1906	Publishes first technical book, *The Bird, Its Form and Function*
1908–09	Travels to Trinidad, Venezuela, and British Guiana
1909–11	Studies pheasants in Asia
1916	Establishes the NYZS's first tropical field station at Kalacoon, in British Guiana
1917–18	Serves in the French Aviation Service during World War I
1918–22	Publishes *A Monograph of the Pheasants* in four volumes
1922	Becomes the director of tropical research for NYZS and continues research on the ecology of the jungle
1925	Explores wildlife in and around the Galápagos using a diving helmet

1927	Studies fish around Haiti
1928	Receives honorary doctorate degrees from Tufts College and Colgate University and publishes *Beneath Tropic Seas*
1930	On June 6, Beebe and Barton complete the first manned descent of the bathysphere to 800 feet (244 m). On June 11, they descend to 1,426 feet (435 m)
1932	NBC broadcasts a dive off Nonsuch Island, Bermuda
1933	The bathysphere is exhibited at the Century of Progress Expedition at Chicago. Beebe and Tee Van publish *Field Book of the Shore Fishes of Bermuda*
1934	On August 15, eebe and Barton set a record dive of 3,028 feet (923 m) off Nonsuch Island, Bermuda
1942	Resumes jungle research in Venezuela and publishes *Book of Bays*
1945	Establishes a jungle research station around Caripito, Venezuela
1950	Builds the Simla Research Station (later renamed the William Beebe Tropical Research Station and now called the Asa Wright Nature Center) in the Arima Valley of Trinidad
1962	Dies on June 4 at age 84

FURTHER READING

Barton, Otis. *The World Beneath the Sea.* New York: Crowell, 1953. Barton's account of his deep ocean explorations and experiences filming marine life.

Beebe, William. *Half Mile Down.* New York: Harcourt, Brace and Company, 1934. Autobiographical account of Beebe's and Barton's dives off Bermuda.

———. *Adventuring with Beebe: Selections from the Writings of William Beebe.* New York: Duell, Sloan, and Pearce, 1955. Contains vividly written passages from Beebe's most popular works.

Garraty, John A., and Mark C. Carnes, eds. *American National Biography*. Vol. 2. New York: Oxford University Press, 1999. Brief account of lives and works of famous Americans in encyclopedia format.

The Official William Beebe Web Site. Available online. URL: http://hometown.aol.com/chines6930/mw1/beebe1.htm. Last updated on January 2, 2005. Includes biographical information, photographs, and a descriptive bibliography of Beebe's works.

Welker, Robert Henry. *Natural Man: The Life of William Beebe*. Bloomington: Indiana University Press, 1975. Most complete story of the man and his accomplishments. Intended for adults, but younger readers could handle this.

Henry Bigelow

(1879-1967)

Henry Bigelow, shown here on the deck of the USS *Grampus*, pioneered an interdisciplinary study of the sea. *(Courtesy of the National Oceanic and Atmospheric Administration/ Department of Commerce)*

The Complex Ecology of the Sea

During the latter half of the 19th century, more information about the oceans was collected than in the previous thousand years. Several famous oceanic expeditions contributed to the knowledge of the physical nature, geology, and life of the sea. Oceanography was a burgeoning field when Henry Bryant Bigelow stumbled into it. Bigelow was a pioneering ocean researcher of the 20th century and was the first to perform a comprehensive study of the Gulf of Maine. Not only did he collect vast amounts of data during his research, but as a result, he also recognized and emphasized the importance of physical, chemical, and biological unity in studying the sea. His recognition for the need to study the complex interdisciplinary nature of the sea led to the establishment of the esteemed *Woods Hole Oceanographic Institution* (WHOI), which has supported leading oceanographic research for 75 years. The many contributions made by Bigelow to marine science earned him the title of father of American oceanography.

From Birds to the Sea

Henry Bryant Bigelow was born to banker Joseph Smith Bigelow and Mary Cleveland Bryant Bigelow on October 3, 1879, in Boston, Massachusetts. As a youth, he often traveled to Europe with his family and developed a love for the outdoors and for sports. The family spent summers at the quaint harbor town of Cohasset, in Massachusetts. Henry graduated from the Milton Academy in 1896 and then took courses at the Massachusetts Institute of Technology while working at the Boston Museum of Natural History. He enrolled at Harvard University in 1897 and graduated cum laude four years later. Though in his memoirs he reported that he did not have much of a social life during college, he made contacts with influential individuals that shaped his career.

Bigelow's early scientific interests were birds. He went on a trip to the Canadian province of Newfoundland and Labrador in 1900. His first scientific publication on the American eider (a northern sea duck with soft down), "A Virginia Record for the American Eider," was published in the respected ornithology journal, *Auk*, in 1901, while he was still an undergraduate. The following year he published a more substantial article, "Birds of the Northeastern Coast of Labrador," also in *Auk*.

In 1901 he was invited to accompany a Harvard professor who was also the director of Harvard's Museum of Comparative Zoology (MCZ), Alexander Agassiz, on an expedition to the oceanic island group the Maldives, located in the Indian Ocean, southwest of Sri Lanka. Bigelow's responsibility was caring for the jellyfish and the siphonophores they collected. He enjoyed the fieldwork during this experience, which sparked an interest in marine invertebrates and taught him the basics of taxonomy, the classification of species. He published papers on the Maldive medusas in 1904 and 1909, establishing himself as a knowledgeable marine biologist. During the period 1904–05, Bigelow traveled to the eastern tropical Pacific with Agassiz, and in 1907, to the West Indies.

In 1904 and 1906, Bigelow earned a master's and a doctorate degree in zoology from Harvard. The topic of Bigelow's doctoral dissertation was the nuclear cycle of *Gonionemus vertens*, a hydrozoan that attaches to eelgrass or sea lettuce using adhesive discs on its tentacles. This experience studying cytology impressed upon Bigelow the necessary discipline for laboratory research.

Bigelow married Elizabeth Perkins Shattuck in 1906, and they eventually had four children together. His wife often accompanied him on his research travels.

The Gulf of Maine

After obtaining his doctorate, Bigelow was given a position as an assistant at Harvard's MCZ, where he cataloged specimens. A visit by John Murray, a Scottish oceanographer who specialized in studying the ocean bottom, prompted Bigelow to investigate the virtually unknown Gulf of Maine. In 1912 he borrowed the schooner *Grampus* from the U.S. Bureau of Fisheries and began an extensive study of the Gulf of Maine that lasted for 12 years and was supported jointly by the MCZ and U.S. Bureau of Fisheries. This work was revolutionary because it was so comprehensive—he studied everything related to the sea in the area. He collected over 10,000 net hauls of marine organisms, sent out over 1,000 drift bottles to study the water's currents and flow, and set up hundreds of stations to measure water temperature and salinity levels. He became an expert on fishes and coelenterates, which are aquatic invertebrates with a radially symmetric saclike body and a single internal cavity. Examples include jellyfish and hydras.

Results from these studies were published in 1924 in three monumental monographs: *Fishes of the Gulf of Maine, Physical Oceanography of the Gulf of Maine,* and *Plankton of the Offshore Waters of the Gulf of Maine.* In the latter, Bigelow described his fortune in having a "veritable *mare incognitum* lay before us" as they set out on

Alexander Agassiz

Henry Bigelow was enticed to enter the field of oceanography by one of the world's leading oceanographers, Swiss-born American Alexander Agassiz (December 17, 1835–March 27, 1910). Agassiz was the son of the renowned zoologist and geologist Louis Agassiz, who demonstrated the existence of a Great Ice Age. The younger Agassiz graduated from Harvard University in 1855 and then pursued studies in engineering at the Lawrence Scientific School of Harvard. He taught at his father's school for women for a while and then traveled to California to participate in a coast survey as a mining engineer.

In 1860 Agassiz returned to Cambridge and started working as an assistant at the Harvard MCZ, which had been established to house his father's extensive zoological specimen collections. Then he worked in Pennsylvania coal mines, managed the Lake Superior copper mines, and visited museums across Europe. Back at Harvard, he became curator of the MCZ upon the death of his father in 1874. In 1885 he resigned as a fellow of Harvard and as curator after having built up an impressive zoological collection. Agassiz established many endowments totaling $1.5 million for Harvard and the MCZ. He assisted C. Wyville Thomson in writing up the reports from the *Challenger* expedition (1872–76) on echinoderms.

the first oceanographic cruise in the Gulf to examine not simply the pelagic fauna but their ecological role, geographical variations, seasonal successions and migrations, and temperature preferences. During these years, Bigelow switched his research focus from cytology and zoology to oceanography and developed an appreciation for the need to understand all of the natural sciences in order to understand the complex cycle of the sea. Throughout his career, he

In 1877 he began intensely research-ing marine life and went on several oceanographic expeditions. Over his career, he voyaged over 100,000 miles and used his engineering back-ground to make many improvements to the dredging, trawling, and two-net equipment. Examinations of ocean cur-rents led to his conclusion that the cur-rents affected the abundance of sur-face plankton. He also demonstrated that deep-sea life was dependent upon plankton and proposed that the Caribbean was a bay of the Pacific Ocean that had been separated during the Cretaceous period, noting that the inhabitant life-forms closely resembled one another. Agassiz authored count-

Alexander Agassiz (right) on the *Albatross*, watching a deep-sea trawl coming to the surface *(Courtesy of the NOAA Central Library)*

less pamphlets, reports, and articles, principally on marine organisms. One notable book, *The Three Cruises of the "Blake,"* summarized data he gath-ered from voyages during the period 1877–80 and included 545 maps and illustrations of the unusual deep-sea life-forms and plankton.

In 1913 the Alexander Agassiz Medal, which is awarded every three years, was established to honor a scientist who has made original contributions to oceanography. Bigelow received this medal in 1931.

would impress this conviction onto his colleagues and students, paving the way for modern oceanography.

In 1919 Bigelow took a temporary break from his Gulf of Maine studies to teach navigational skills and serve as a navigation officer aboard the U.S. Army Transport, *Amphion*. He also assisted the U.S. Shipping Board and consulted the U.S. Coast Guard for the International Ice Patrol. From examinations of the plankton drifting,

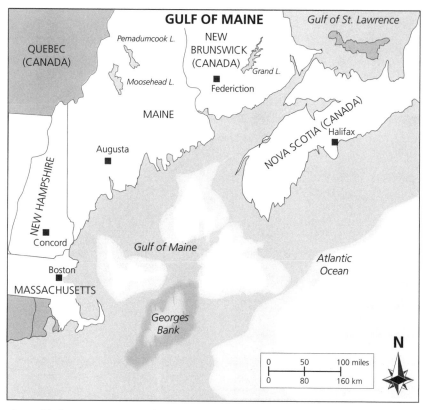

The Gulf of Maine connects the New England states of Massachusetts, New Hampshire, and Maine and the Canadian provinces New Brunswick and Nova Scotia with 36,000 square miles (93,240 sq km) of ocean, 7,500 miles (12,070 km) of shoreline, and roughly 5,000 islands.

surface temperatures, and salinity, he drew conclusions about drifting icebergs. The hydrography knowledge he gained was ultimately beneficial to his research. Bigelow accepted a teaching appointment at Harvard in 1921.

Complex Ecology of the Sea

As secretary for the Committee on Oceanography of the National Academy of Sciences (NAS), Bigelow composed a report titled "On the Scope, Problems, and Economic Importance of the Oceanography, on the Present Situation in America, and on the

Handicaps to Development, with Suggested Remedies" in 1929. This well-received, influential report was made public in the form of a book, *Oceanography, Its Scope, Problems, and Economic Importance* (1931). In his report, Bigelow portrayed oceanography as a youthful field and defined it in terms of three chief subdivisions: geological, physical-chemical, and biological. He recommended that oceanographers be grounded in the principles of all three disciplines, for which he provided overviews summarizing the current knowledge. In portions of this report that were not published, Bigelow made specific recommendations for how to best resolve the current deficiencies in the state of oceanographic research in the United States. To substantiate the recommendations, Bigelow described the applications of oceanography and discussed the economic ramifications of improved research in the mentioned areas. WHOI was established based on Bigelow's report, and the Rockefeller Foundation donated $2.5 million. In addition, the Scripps Institution, the University of Washington, and the Bermuda Biological Station received financial assistance.

WHOI and Harvard

Bigelow served as the first director of WHOI from 1930 to 1939. He made daily rounds, making himself accessible to his scientists, and he requested that his staff perform field research at least once a year. The vessel *Atlantis* was made available for them to do so. Bigelow successfully recruited eminent biologists, chemists, and physical geologists without worrying whether or not they had already studied oceanography. He was more concerned with attracting clever, creative scientists who were willing to apply their talents to oceanography. Today, WHOI remains dedicated to research and education in the marine sciences and is the largest independent oceanographic institution in the world. Although Bigelow resigned as director of WHOI in 1940, he maintained a close association with the institute by serving as president of the corporation (1940–50) and then chairman of the board of trustees (1950–60).

In the early 1940s, Bigelow researched Georges Bank from the *Atlantis*. Fishermen depended on this region for haddock, thus scientists were exploring the cause for its long phytoplankton season compared to that of the Gulf of Maine. In 1947 Bigelow published *Wind Waves at Sea, Breakers, and Surf,* which served as an introduction to waves for the U.S. Navy. Written with W.T. Edmondson, the text summarized the physical nature of wind waves, wave dimensions and contours, and the effect of waves on small vessels.

Bigelow served as editor-in-chief of the series *Fishes of the Western North Atlantic* (1948–64), a cooperative publication written for *ichthyologists* as well as general naturalists. In collaboration with William C. Schroeder, Bigelow contributed more than 40 papers on ichthyology between 1948 and 1965.

At Harvard, Bigelow had been appointed a lecturer (1921), associate professor of zoology (1927), professor of zoology (1931), and the Alexander Agassiz Professor of Zoology (1944). Bigelow retired as a professor emeritus from Harvard in 1950, but he continued serving on the faculty for the MCZ until his death. He had served as curator for coelenterates (1913–25), research curator (1925–27), and curator of oceanography (1927–50). When Bigelow jokingly suggested, in 1960, that the university show their appreciation for his lengthy tenure, the president of Harvard presented him with a bottle of bourbon whiskey.

Bigelow had served on several influential committees and did not shy away from administrative functions: the National Research Council Committee on Oceanography (1919–23), the National Research Council Committee on Submarine Configuration, for which he served as vice-chairman (1930–32), and the NAS Committee on Oceanography, for which he was secretary (1928–34) and chairman (1934–38).

Bigelow was the distinguished recipient of numerous medals and honors and was elected to membership of numerous academic organizations. WHOI established a chair in oceanography in his name in 1958. WHOI's board of trustees established the Henry Bryant Bigelow Award, WHOI's highest honor, for those who make significant inquiries into the phenomena of the sea. The first recipient of the medal and cash prize was Bigelow himself in 1960. He also received the Alexander Agassiz Medal of the NAS (1931). Several universities awarded Bigelow honorary doctorate degrees during his lifetime.

Henry Bigelow died on December 11, 1967, at his home in Concord, Massachusetts. A laboratory at WHOI bears his name, as does a marine research institution in West Boothbay Harbor, Maine, which was established in 1974. In 1970 the U.S. Department of the Interior named a bay in the Gulf of Maine, located between Cape Ann and Cape Small, Bigelow Bight.

For the vast amount of information he collected concerning various forms of marine life and for his comprehensive study of the Gulf of Maine, Bigelow is considered a pioneer in oceanography. Before the 1930s, the field was merely an assemblage of facts and data—lists of identified fauna, maps of ocean depths at different positions, and locations and directions of currents. Bigelow encouraged oceanographers to synthesize all the gathered information by embracing the different fields of biology, chemistry, and physical geology to find the connections. This effort for unification gave oceanography an ecological aim that has persisted into the 21st century. Alfred C. Redfield, in his memoir written for the NAS, summarized Bigelow's contributions to oceanography,

Not only did a man emerge who had prepared himself, perhaps unwittingly, for leadership at a time when men of influence sensed that something should be done to improve the status of marine science in America, but new ideas were in the air, wafted across the ocean from a multitude of general scientific advances. Henry Bigelow, though trained in the classical tradition, was sensitive to these breezes, wise enough to grasp their implication, and bold enough to act on their meaning.

CHRONOLOGY

1879	Henry Bigelow is born on October 3 in Boston, Massachusetts
1896	Works and studies at the Boston Museum of Natural History
1897–1901	Attends Harvard University
1901	Publishes first scientific paper, "A Virginia Record for the American Eider," in *Auk*

1901–02	Bigelow accompanies Alexander Agassiz on an expedition to the Maldive Islands
1904	Receives a master's degree in zoology from Harvard University
1904–05	Accompanies Agassiz on the *Albatross* expedition to the eastern Pacific
1906	Receives a doctorate degree in zoology from Harvard University and is appointed assistant at Harvard's
1911	Publishes a famous paper on siphonophores
1912–24	Engages in an extensive study of the Gulf of Maine
1913	Is appointed curator of coelenterates for the MCZ
1919–23	Serves as a member of the National Research Council Committee on Oceanography
1924	Publishes three monographs as a result of his 12-year study of the Gulf of Maine: *Fishes of the Gulf of Maine, Plankton of the Offshore Waters of the Gulf of Maine,* and *Physical Oceanography of the Gulf of Maine*
1925	Is promoted to research curator at the MCZ
1927	Is appointed associate professor of zoology at Harvard University and curator of oceanography at the MCZ
1930–40	Serves as the first director of WHOI
1931	Bigelow is promoted to full professor at Harvard and publishes a report for the NAS, made public in book form, *Oceanography, Its Scope, Problems, and Economic Importance*
1940–50	Serves as president of the corporation for WHOI
1944	Is appointed Alexander Agassiz Professor of Zoology at Harvard University
1947	Publishes *Wind Waves at Sea, Breakers, and Surf*
1950	Retires as a professor emeritus from Harvard
1950–60	Serves as chairman of the board of trustees for WHOI

| **1962** | Formally retires from the MCZ faculty but continues working for them until his death |
| **1967** | Dies on December 11 at his home in Concord, Massachusetts |

FURTHER READING

Bigelow, Henry Bryant. *Oceanography; Its Scope, Problems, and Economic Importance.* Boston and New York: Houghton Mifflin, 1931. Bigelow's description of the developing field of oceanography that led to the establishment of WHOI.

Bigelow Laboratory for Ocean Sciences. Available online. URL: http://www.bigelow.org. Accessed on January 17, 2004. Search the Web site for "Henry Bigelow" for links to information on Bigelow and current research performed by the lab.

Biographical Memoirs. Vol. 48. Washington, D.C.: National Academy of Sciences, 1976. Fullest memoir of Bigelow, written by a distinguished colleague for the premier scientific organization of the United States.

Garraty, John A., and Mark C. Carnes, eds. *American National Biography.* Vol. 2. New York: Oxford University Press, 1999. Brief account of lives and works of famous Americans in encyclopedia format.

Woods Hole Oceanographic Institution. Available online. URL: http://www.whoi.edu. Accessed on January 17, 2005. The home page for WHOI contains links to information about the institution, its research programs, and its history.

5

Ernest Everett Just

(1883-1941)

Ernest Just was a world authority on the fertilization and development of marine organisms. *(Marine Biological Laboratory Archives)*

Marine Invertebrate Embryologist

When the Marine Biological Laboratory (MBL) at Woods Hole, Massachusetts, was founded in 1888, it helped launch a new era in marine science by providing a geographically isolated haven where the best students, teachers, and researchers could come to explore the structure and mechanisms of life without distraction. The benefits were enormous, as knowledge gained through the efforts of the MBL community has improved the understanding of ecosystems, neurobiology, reproductive biology, and molecular evolution to name a few. Many distinguished scientists can claim MBL heritage, including a 20th-century researcher named Ernest Everett Just, who overcame racial discrimination to become a pioneering marine biologist. He was an expert in marine invertebrate zoology who made important discoveries and taught others how to do the same in the areas of *fertilization*, parthenogenesis, and early embryology. As an accomplished cellular physiologist, one who studies the functions and activities of living organisms at the cellular level, he recognized and called attention to the role of protoplasm in cellular development.

Opportunity in Education

Ernest Everett Just was born on August 14, 1883, to Charles and Mary Cooper Just in Charleston, South Carolina. He was their fourth child, born into unfortunate circumstances. His father was an alcoholic who could not keep a job and died penniless when Ernest was only four years old. Several of his siblings died young, and his family moved to St. James Island, South Carolina. His mother labored in the phosphate mines to support her family, dedicated herself to improving the education of the mostly black islanders, and taught Sunday school and dressmaking in her home. She was such a devoted member of the community that the town became known as Maryville in her honor. As the oldest surviving child, Ernest shared many of the routine household chores, such as cooking, cleaning, and caring for his younger siblings, but he never complained about the extra work.

Until age 12, Ernest attended the school his mother ran, the Frederick Deming, Jr. Industrial School. In 1896 he enrolled at a black high school, the Colored Normal, Industrial, Agricultural and Mechanical College, in Orangeburg, South Carolina, to be trained as a teacher. He received his license to teach in the black public schools in 1899, but at only 15 years old, he was not ready to devote his life to a career in teaching. Because the high school he attended did not adequately prepare him for college, he looked at reputable northern schools. He received a scholarship to attend Kimball Union Academy in Meriden, New Hampshire, and worked on a ship to earn passage to New York in 1900. At Kimball, Ernest was the editor-in-chief for the school newspaper and excelled at oratory. He completed high school in three years instead of the usual four and was accepted to Dartmouth College in Hanover, New Hampshire.

Just was initially not happy at Dartmouth. Everyone seemed more excited about football than academics, whereas he was committed to learning and preparing for his future. After becoming excited by reading an essay on the development of an egg cell during his sophomore year, Just eagerly signed up for every biology course the college offered, but he also excelled at the classics and earned the highest freshman grade in Greek. The head of the biology department, William Patten, asked Just to assist him in writing and illustrating the section on frog embryonic development for a textbook he was writing, *The Evolution of the Vertebrates and Their Kin* (1912). Twice during college, Just was awarded the title of Rufus Choate Scholar, the highest academic award for an undergraduate at Dartmouth, and was elected into Phi Beta Kappa, the nation's oldest academic honor society. He earned a bachelor's degree in zoology and two minors in Greek and history, graduating magna cum laude in 1907.

Doctoral Research on Sandworms

Just wanted to obtain a research position, but such jobs were not available to blacks. He headed to Washington, D.C., where he accepted an instructorship in English and rhetoric at Howard University, a historically black private university. His pupils were fortunate to have a dedicated and enthusiastic teacher. A few years later Just was appointed an assistant professor of biology, teaching zoology and histology. In 1912 he was promoted to full professor and head of the zoology department and later taught in and headed the physiology department at the medical school. Just also involved himself in other aspects of campus life. He organized a drama club for the students and acted as adviser to a new black fraternity, Omega Psi Phi. He remained associated with Howard University until his death.

Desirous of a graduate degree, Just asked his former professor, Patten, for advice regarding graduate training. Patten suggested he

Frank Rattray Lillie

Frank Rattray Lillie (June 27, 1870–November 5, 1947) graduated from the University of Toronto in 1891 and attended a summer course at the recently founded MBL at Woods Hole, Massachusetts. This visit began an association that lasted for 54 years. He earned his doctorate degree in zoology from the University of Chicago in 1894, and then taught at the University of Michigan and Vassar College before becoming an assistant professor of embryology at the University of Chicago in 1900. In 1900 Lillie also became assistant director of MBL and was director from 1908 to 1930. Since MBL was primarily a summer laboratory at the time, Lillie returned to the University of Chicago during the academic year where he became head of the biology department and dean of zoology.

Lillie's research focused on mussel development, and his excitement about embryology persists even today at MBL. In 1908 he published a leading embryology textbook, *The Development of the Chick.* He is also famous for his studies on freemartin calves. Freemartins are infertile females born as a twin to a male. Lillie examined the cause for infertility in the females and determined it was the result of exposure to hormones secreted in utero by the male fetus that prevented normal development of the female reproductive system.

Respected by his colleagues, Lillie served as chair of the National Academy of Sciences and the National Research Council. Lillie secured a $3 million grant from the Rockefeller Foundation to help establish the Woods Hole Oceanographic Institution (WHOI) in 1930. He served as president of the WHOI board of directors for nine years. WHOI has since become the largest oceanographic institution in the world.

contact Frank R. Lillie, the head of the department of zoology at the University of Chicago and the director of the MBL at Woods Hole, Massachusetts. Lillie invited Just to come to MBL, an independent research and teaching institution not affiliated with any university, as his research assistant for the summer of 1909, the first of many summers Just would spend at MBL. He advanced his knowledge of theoretical biology by enrolling in an invertebrate zoology course that first summer and embryology the following year. With Lillie, he researched sandworm fertilization, the process where male and female *gametes* unite to form a *zygote*, a fertilized egg. Impressed by Just's intelligence and dedication, Lillie recommended that Just enroll in a doctoral program at the University of Chicago in absentia.

The polychaete *Nereis* is a segmented worm that can grow up to six inches (15 cm) in length and lives in sandy or rocky beaches, estuaries, mud flats, and wharfs. Because they have unique breeding patterns, studying fertilization in *Nereis* was a difficult process. Just was convinced, rightly, that the condition of his research material was paramount to obtaining reliable and meaningful results. The

Sandworms are polychaetes, a class of annelids or segmented worms, that are mostly marine. Each segment has a pair of flaps that function in respiration and movement. *(Courtesy of the Photo Collection of Dr. James P. McVey, NOAA Sea Grant Program)*

eggs he studied needed to be fresh, and they could only live for 24 hours outside the female's body. The sandworms swarmed only at nighttime, monthly, in cycle with the Moon. Just knew when and where he needed to collect his specimens using a hand net and a lantern. Sandworm fertilization is an external process, meaning the eggs and the sperm are shed into the water, and fertilization occurs there rather than inside the body as it does in mammals. Just had to bring the fertilized cells to the lab quickly and make his observations throughout the night. Sometimes he captured male and female worms separately and brought them back to the lab. He perfected a method for artificial fertilization by washing and drying off the male sandworms, then cutting them open to collect dry sperm cells. Since female worms only release eggs naturally in the presence of males, he would slice open a washed female to release the eggs and then mix the cell types while observing the process under a microscope.

A Growing Reputation

In 1911 Just made an important discovery that cemented his status as a marine invertebrate zoologist. He was examining cell *cleavage*, the process of early embryonic development in which the cell membrane pinches off, followed by repeated cell division, converting the zygote into a ball of cells. He discovered that the location of sperm entrance together with the polar bodies determined the position of the line of cleavage. These results were published in "The Relation of the First Cleavage Plane to the Entrance Point of Sperm" in *The Biological Bulletin* in 1912. During the next two years, he published two additional articles on breeding habits of sandworms.

In 1912 Just married Ethel Highwarden, a German teacher and the daughter of an Ohio riverboat captain. They bought a Victorian three-story house in Le Droit Park, a residential section in northwest Washington, D.C., and filled it with three children.

The summer he got married, Just met biologist Jacques Loeb from the Rockefeller Institute for Medical Research. Loeb was committed to improving black education, specifically in the field of medicine. He became involved with the National Association for the Advancement of Colored People (NAACP), and when asked to recommend a recipient for a new award for an American of African descent "who shall have made the highest achievement during the preceding year in an honorable field of human endeavor," he suggested Just. The governor of New York, Charles Whitman, presented Just with the first Spingarn Medal in 1915.

While the publicity and national recognition from this award did much to advance his reputation as a scientist, Just knew he needed a Ph.D. to further advance his career. In 1915 he moved to Chicago for one year, leaving his wife and first daughter behind while he completed residency and minor course requirements. Lillie accepted Just's previous publications as his doctoral thesis, and the following year Just received a doctorate in zoology, the study of animal life, from the University of Chicago.

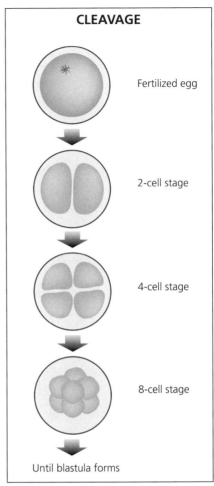

CLEAVAGE

Fertilized egg

2-cell stage

4-cell stage

8-cell stage

Until blastula forms

Cleavage is a series of rapid cell divisions that occur following fertilization, converting a single fertilized egg into a ball of many cells.

After earning his doctorate, Just was recommended for and elected to membership in many professional societies, including the American Society of Naturalists, the American Society of Zoologists (for which he served as president), the American Association for the Advancement of Science, and the American Ecological Society. At the time, this was quite an achievement for a black scientist. He resumed his routine of teaching at Howard during the school year and researching at Woods Hole during the summers. Eventually, Just became a member of the corporation of the MBL and for a while served as editor of the laboratory's journal, *The Biological Bulletin*. He later served as associate editor for several other scientific journals, including *Physiological Zoology* and the *Journal of Morphology*.

Sand Dollar Fertilization

During the period 1917–19, Just researched the fertilization process in the sand dollar, *Echinarachnius parma*. After the sperm contacts the egg, the two cellular membranes fuse, and a series of changes that alter the outer portion of the egg cytoplasm take place. This is necessary to prevent polyspermy, fertilization by more than one sperm, and also results in biochemical changes in the cytoplasm. Just published a series of articles in *The Biological Bulletin* (1919–20) describing his research on fertilization and activation of the biochemical changes in the egg. These investigations led Just to discoveries that contradicted some of Loeb's conclusions about parthenogenesis, the process whereby an unfertilized egg develops into an adult organism. Loeb had pioneered research in the study of parthenogenesis and was able to induce development in sea urchin and frog eggs without any sperm by pricking them with a needle or treating them with very salty water. Loeb proposed a double theory of cytolysis and correction, where a cytolytic factor broke down the outer surface of the egg and a corrective factor prevented the cytolysis from going too far. He initiated cytolysis artificially by treating eggs with salt water and butyric acid and then stopped cytolysis by rinsing away the butyric acid with salt water or adding magnesium. Since Loeb could re-create fertilization in the lab by chemical simulation, he concluded that fertilization was a nonspecific process, similar to artificial parthenogenesis. Just found that normal development could also be induced by treating the eggs in the reverse order, using the supposed corrective agent first and then the cytolytic agent, or even by treatment with very salty water by itself! Just also examined the physiological condition and degree of activation of the eggs following butyric acid treatment and concluded that Loeb either had poor laboratory technique or a general lack of knowledge about the initiation of development. Just had been studying reproduction in marine invertebrates for over a decade by this time, and other scientists respected his technical expertise in this area. His advice on how to discern normally developing eggs from abnormal ones was sought and trusted by embryologists at MBL and elsewhere. While this research soured the relationship between Just and Loeb, it established Just as an outstanding researcher. Lillie invited Just to collaborate with him in writing the fertilization section of E. V. Cowdry's *General Cytology* (1924) book. Lillie proudly introduced Just to philanthropist Julius Rosenwald in 1920. Rosenwald felt that because of Just's race, he was being denied the advantages that accompany an academic

FERTILIZATION

In marine invertebrates, following contact with a sperm cell, a fertilization membrane forms, preventing penetration by additional sperm.

appointment at a major academic institution and offered a grant to Just to help fund his research. This initiated a series of grants that supported Just's research until the mid-1930s and allowed him to relinquish his teaching responsibilities at the medical school in 1920 to devote more time to his research. Over time, he began to view his teaching responsibilities at Howard as a burden and looked for opportunities to do research elsewhere. Being black, however, eliminated the possibility of finding a research professorship at a predominantly white institution.

Escape from Racism

Even though MBL offered Just a place to perform his pioneering research and a break from his heavy teaching load at Howard, he faced racial discrimination there. When he was finally able to convince his wife and children to accompany him to Woods Hole during the summer of 1927, they were treated so horrifically that Just had to interrupt his research to move them back to Washington, D.C., after only a few weeks. Howard University was not a research institution, so Just could not carry out his experiments there. By 1929, frustrated with the environment at Howard and racial oppression in the United States, Just began traveling to Europe to attend scientific meetings and to study. In 1929 he worked as a guest researcher at the Naples Zoological Station, extending fertilization principles he discovered on American marine organisms to species that inhabited the European waters. He repeated experiments he had performed on *Echinarachnius* (sand dollar) and *Arbacia* (sea urchin) on European species *Paracentrotus lividus* and *Echinus microtuberculatus*. Two decades before, he had observed differences in breeding habits between the American and European sandworms, which some scientists believed to be the same species. In Naples, he carefully examined the two and distinguished *Platynereis megalops* and *Nereis dumerilii* as distinct species. As a break from the more tedious fertilization studies that had to be carried out under a microscope, Just performed anatomical studies of the wormlike chordate *Amphioxus*, also known as a lancelet.

Over the next decade, Just visited several other European scientific facilities. In 1930 he was the first American invited as a guest professor to do research in Berlin at the highly regarded Kaiser Wilhelm Institute for Biology, where he studied the function of the ectoplasm in the freshwater *protozoan Amoeba proteus*. He worked at the Laboratoire d'Anatomie et d'Histologie Comparées at the University of Paris and the Station Biologique de Roscoff at the Sorbonne.

Just was welcomed by the scientific community and drawn to the culture of Europe. Though he returned to Woods Hole to celebrate Lillie's 60th birthday, he never returned there to work. From time to time he returned to Howard University to teach or perform compulsory administrative tasks, but he was always anxious to get back overseas. After coming to a minimally satisfactory agreement with Howard's administration concerning his salary support, which they wanted to discontinue in 1938, Just exiled himself to Paris.

Magnum Opus

Just composed *The Biology of the Cell Surface* (1939), a textbook that summarized the results of two decades of his research. One of Just's major contributions was dispelling the assumption that all cellular activities were controlled by the nucleus of the cell. He demonstrated that the cytoplasm, the material outside of the nucleus but still contained within the cell, also performed important cellular functions. He asserted that the ectoplasm, the outer, rigid layer of protoplasm, the essential semifluid living substance of cells, played an important role in fertilization and embryonic development. Just found that polyspermy, the condition of penetration by more than one sperm, resulted from an improperly functioning ectoplasm. In addition to his research on fertilization, egg activation, and cell division, Just made other contributions, including studies examining the effect of ultraviolet radiation on the number of chromosomes in eggs and the hydration and dehydration of cells.

In 1940 he published *Basic Methods for Experiments on Eggs of Marine Animals*, a handbook of laboratory techniques that outlined methods for handling egg and sperm cells from 28 marine species. He also stressed the need for using clean glassware and shared his knowledge about temperature and handling that would maintain the healthy condition of specimens in the lab.

Just divorced his wife in 1939 and married Hedwig Schnetzler, a graduate student in philosophy that he met in Berlin and with whom he had been having an affair for eight years. In 1940 Just was forced from his laboratory by the Nazis who had taken over France, and he and his part-Jewish wife struggled to obtain the necessary papers for passage to America. He brought his then pregnant wife to Washington, D.C., where he resumed teaching at Howard and began writing a manuscript, "Ethics and the Struggle for Existence." Their daughter was born in 1940. Just's health began to fail, and in the summer of 1941, Just was diagnosed with pancreatic cancer. He died on October 27, 1941, at the age of 58, in Washington, D.C., and was buried in the Lincoln Cemetery.

Just was a quiet, bookish, dignified man, who published over 60 scientific articles in addition to his two textbooks in his short lifetime. His contributions are still remembered and have been honored in recent years. In 1983 the 26th Southeastern Conference of Developmental Biology dedicated to Just a symposium on cellular and molecular biology of invertebrate development at the Bell W. Branch Institute for the Marine Biology and Coastal Research in South Carolina. In 1996 the U.S. Post Office issued a stamp in his honor. Recognized as a world authority on marine organisms, Just made significant advances to the field of invertebrate zoology, especially concerning fertilization and early embryonic development. The findings of this research carry over to human studies, for which marine organisms are excellent simple models, and have contributed to the development of techniques such as in vitro fertilization. Whether intended or not, by choosing to pursue the rational, objective field of science in the face of discrimination, Just also made progress in the great effort to reach equality among races in America.

CHRONOLOGY

1883	Ernest Everett Just is born on August 14 in Charleston, South Carolina
1903	Graduates from Kimball Union Academy
1907	Receives a bachelor's degree in zoology from Dartmouth College and starts teaching English at Howard University
1909	Begins graduate training at the MBL at Woods Hole, Massachusetts
1912	Publishes first scientific paper, "The Relation of the First Cleavage Plane to the Entrance Point of Sperm" in *The Biological Bulletin* and is promoted to full professor and head of the zoology department at Howard University

1915	The NAACP awards Just the first Spingarn Medal for performing a "foremost service to his race"
1916	Receives a doctorate degree in zoology from the University of Chicago
1919–20	Publishes a series of articles about fertilization and egg activation in *The Biological Bulletin*
1920	Receives external support that allows him to quit teaching at Howard's medical school and devote more time to his research
1929–40	Studies at research institutions in Italy, Germany, and France
1939	Publishes *The Biology of the Cell Surface,* summarizing his research from the 1920s and 1930s
1940	Just publishes *Basic Methods for Experiments on Eggs of Marine Animals.* He was forced out of his lab in Paris and returned to Howard University briefly
1941	Dies of pancreatic cancer on October 27 in Washington, D.C., at age 58

FURTHER READING

Brown, Mitchell C. "The Faces of Science: African Americans in the Sciences." Princeton University. Available online. URL: http://www.princeton.edu/~mcbrown/display/faces.html. Last updated on February 21, 2004. Profiles African-American men and women who have contributed to the advancement of science and engineering, includes memberships and bibliography.

Garraty, John A., and Mark C. Carnes, eds. *American National Biography.* Vol. 12. New York: Oxford University Press, 1999. Brief account of lives and works of famous Americans in encyclopedia format.

Krapp, Kristine M., ed. *Notable Black American Scientists.* Detroit: Gale Research, 1999. Brief biographies of approximately 250 black Americans who have made contributions to the sciences.

Manning, Kenneth R. *Black Apollo of Science: The Life of Ernest Everett Just.* New York: Oxford University Press, 1983. Full-length, standard biography that explores Just's background and personal life as well as accomplishments.

Polking, Kirk. *Oceanographers and Explorers of the Sea.* Springfield, N.J.: Enslow, 1999. Profiles 10 marine scientists whose specialties range from biology to physical geology. Appropriate for middle and high school students.

Smith, Jessie Carney, ed. *Black Heroes.* Detroit: Visible Ink Press, 2001. Profiles 150 individuals who have significantly influenced black American culture, not limited to scientists.

Harry Hammond Hess

6

(1906–1969)

Harry Hammond Hess proposed a model for seafloor spreading that developed into the theory of plate tectonics. *(Courtesy of Archives, Department of Geosciences, Princeton University)*

Model of Seafloor Spreading

The beginning of this millennium has found scientists depending on techniques developed by oceanographers to study extraterrestrial oceans in our solar system. Just as pioneers in oceanography had to develop methods for probing miles beneath what can be directly observed at the Earth's surface, the National Aeronautics and Space Administration (NASA) currently is developing techniques for exploring possible oceans deep under miles of ice on the moons of Jupiter and Saturn. In the 1960s, NASA began forging this relationship between oceanography and space science when they appointed a foremost marine geologist as principal investigator of recovered moon rocks. Harry Hammond Hess is best known for formulating a theory on the origin and evolution of ocean basins. Based on observations from which Alfred Wegener proposed his theory of continental drift in 1912, Hess visualized a process occurring deep below the oceanic crust that caused seafloor spreading. In this model, the seafloor is created at ridges and sinks at *trenches* back into the Earth's mantle. This concept provided a model that catapulted the plate tectonics theory into the Earth sciences mainstream.

The Little Admiral

Harry Hammond Hess was born on May 24, 1906, in New York City, to Julian and Elizabeth Engel Hess. His father worked at the New York Stock Exchange. Harry grew up with one brother named Frank. When he was five, Harry's parents photographed him in a sailor suit and fittingly titled the portrait, "The Little Admiral," foreshadowing Harry's career. He attended Asbury Park High School in New Jersey, where he specialized in foreign languages.

In 1923 Hess enrolled at Yale University where he planned to major in electrical engineering. He changed his major to geology and received a bachelor's degree in 1927. A mining company, Loangwa Concessions, Ltd., hired Hess to perform exploratory geological mapping and to look for mineral deposits in Africa. He did not enjoy this work very much because he had to survey where he was told rather than where he believed he would find something valuable. After two years, he came back to the United States to attend graduate school, but this experience had taught him to appreciate the importance of fieldwork in geological research.

As a doctoral candidate at Princeton University, he learned about mineralogy (the study of minerals, their identification, distribution, and properties), petrology (the study of the origin, composition, and structure of rocks), and the structure of the ocean basin. In 1931 he accompanied Dutch geophysicist Felix Andries Vening

Meinesz on a mission to carry out gravity measurements in the West Indies and the Bahamas. Information about gravity at different positions over the Earth's surface gives geologists insight into the composition of the rock under the surface because gravitational fields are stronger over areas with greater mass, which are denser. The measurements had to be performed within a submarine because a pendulum system was used, and ships moved around too much from the surface waves and wind. One interesting observation from this voyage was that the gravity over the Caribbean trench was much weaker than expected. A trench is a long, narrow furrow along the edges of the ocean floor, thus, the gravity was expected to be weaker, as it is over all valleys, but the extreme weakness told Hess and Vening Meinesz that the underlying structure was unusual. Scientists were aware that volcanoes were often located along trenches and that earthquakes occurred nearby. Hess wondered about the implications of this finding.

Hess obtained a Ph.D. in geology in 1932. His dissertation was on the serpentinization of a large *peridotite* intrusive located in the Blue Ridge Mountains of Virginia. A peridotite is a type of *igneous rock* containing the minerals olivine and pyroxene, and *intrusive* means that the rock formed as magma without reaching the surface of the Earth. Serpentinization of peridotites is a chemical process by which the minerals olivine and pyroxene change to the mineral serpentine. The peridotite rock is changed into serpentinite, a rock composed of the mineral serpentine. Hess remained interested in mineralogy throughout his career and published two papers, "Pyroxenes of Common Mafic Magmas" (1941) and "Stillwater Igneous Complex, Montana" (1960), that both became classics in the field. NASA later named Hess the principal investigator for pyroxene studies of moon rock samples.

After receiving his doctorate, Hess taught at Rutgers from 1932 to 1933 and then worked as a research associate at the Geophysical Laboratory of the Carnegie Institution of Washington, D.C., for one year. He obtained a teaching position in geology at Princeton in 1934 and remained associated with Princeton until 1966. The same year he joined Princeton he married Annette Burns, and they eventually had two sons together, George and Frank.

From the Atlantic to the Pacific

Hess had joined the U.S. Navy as a lieutenant in order to facilitate operations on a Navy submarine that he used for gravity studies following his research with Vening Meinesz. He was in the naval reserves when Pearl Harbor was attacked on December 7, 1941. Hess reported for active duty the next morning. Because he had submarine experience, he became an antisubmarine warfare officer with the responsibility of detecting enemy submarine operations patterns in the north Atlantic. Hess advised the U.S. Navy that German submarines might be using the cloud cover north of the Gulf Stream (a current that runs from the Gulf of Mexico up the U.S. Atlantic coastline) to escape detection during surfacing. This suggestion resulted in the clearing out of submarines in the north Atlantic within one year.

Hess took advantage of his time in the navy by patterning the travel routes in order to facilitate his studies on the geology of the ocean floor. He installed a deep-sea echo sounder on his transport ship and continuously used it. This piece of equipment was used to measure the depth of the sea bottom over which the ship traveled by sending out a sound signal downward from the ship and measuring the time it took for the signal to bounce back from the ocean floor. Using this data, Hess constructed *bathymetric maps* that showed the contours of the ocean floor across a large area of the Pacific Ocean. While collecting bathymetric data, Hess discovered flat-topped underwater volcanoes that he named *guyots* after Swiss geologist Arnold Guyot, who had founded the department of geology at Princeton University in 1854. Hess remained in the naval reserves until his death, attaining the rank of rear admiral in 1961.

Baffling Marine Geology Discoveries

In July 1950, a group of scientists studying the seafloor of the Pacific Ocean made some surprising discoveries that influenced the formulation of Hess's developing ideas about the origin and evolution of ocean basins. Scientists believed that the oceanic crust was mostly flat and extremely thick due to the accumulation of billions of years of sediment from continental erosion. Using explosives and seismic waves, the crew determined the thickness of the oceanic crust to be about 4 miles (7 km). This was much thinner than expected, since the continental crust was known to be about five times thicker. Geologists thought the oceans had existed for four billion years, so why was there so little accumulated sediment? The crew took samples from guyots and were surprised to find coral rather than rocky sand, as anticipated. Coral is usually found in shallow areas, and some guyots are two miles (3.2 km) underwater. Also, it proved to be approximately 130 million years old, hundreds of millions of years younger than expected. Fossil evidence further confirmed the relatively young age of the ocean floor.

A few years later, American oceanographer Maurice Ewing observed that oceanic ridges, underground mountain ranges, have *rifts*, or valleys, running through their centers. The seam of the rift appeared to be due to splitting apart, which was interesting because, in contrast, terrestrial mountain ranges were believed to arise from compression, from chunks of land being forced together. The presence of lava and absence of sediment along the ridges also baffled scientists.

Proposal of Seafloor Spreading

Hess contemplated these many unexpected discoveries in relation to the theory of continental drift proposed by German meteorologist and geophysicist Alfred Wegener in 1912. After noticing that the east coast of South America and the west coast of Africa fit together like pieces of a jigsaw puzzle and collecting additional fossil evidence, Wegener concluded that the continents had once been connected but split and drifted thousands of miles apart. Wegener offered no explanation for the mechanism driving continental drift, but Hess modified Wegener's theory and provided a plausible driving force. Wegener thought that drifting continents somehow plowed through the ocean floor, but Hess believed they rode along passively as the ocean floor was carried away from its ridges.

In 1960 Hess first proposed his theory of seafloor spreading. In doing so, he explained the *mid-oceanic ridge* splitting, the presence of lava surrounding ridges, and the thinness of the oceanic crust. The attractive model suggested that the oceanic crust was indeed splitting at a seam, the rift in the center of the mid-oceanic ridge. As it split, melted magma rose through these weak areas and erupted as lava from the spreading ridges, forming new crust composed mostly of basalt as it cooled. The newly formed crust then was carried away by the mantle spreading out laterally beneath the crust, away from the ridge where it would eventually dive back beneath the surface of the Earth at trenches, located along faults formed by compression. At the trenches, slabs of crust would be forced under other slabs of crust, back into the Earth's mantle.

Hess proposed *convection,* heat transfer by fluid motion, as the driving force behind the process of seafloor spreading. The mantle, located just underneath the crust, is solid rock formed mostly from iron and magnesium minerals, but just below the surface it may melt into magma, which cools into the igneous rock basalt. Though solid, the molten mantle can flow slowly like a fluid, forming convection cells. The hotter rock is less dense and rises, and as the rock cools, it sinks. When it cools and sinks, it pulls the overlaying crust down into the mantle with it. The crust that disappeared into the trenches was constantly replenished by newly erupted lava at the ridge. Hess called this paper "an essay in geopoetry" and issued preprints of it in 1960. The official paper, titled "History of Ocean Basins," was published in 1962 by the Geological Society of America in a symposium volume called *Petrologic Studies: A Volume in Honor of A. F. Buddington.* Buddington had been Hess's petrology professor at Princeton and became a close friend.

Hess's paper was well received, and additional paleomagnetic evidence supporting his theory of seafloor spreading soon came out. *Paleomagnetism* is the science of reconstruction of the Earth's ancient magnetic field and the positions of the continents from the evidence of magnetization in ancient rocks. Because the Earth acts like a giant spherical magnet, rocks containing iron-rich minerals are magnetized in alignment with the Earth's poles. When magnetic rocks solidify, they become a permanent indicator of the direction of the Earth's magnetic field at the time of their solidification. Every few million years, the Earth's poles reverse, thus the age of the rocks and their direction of magnetization provide geophysicists with information regarding the history of the direction of the Earth's magnetic poles.

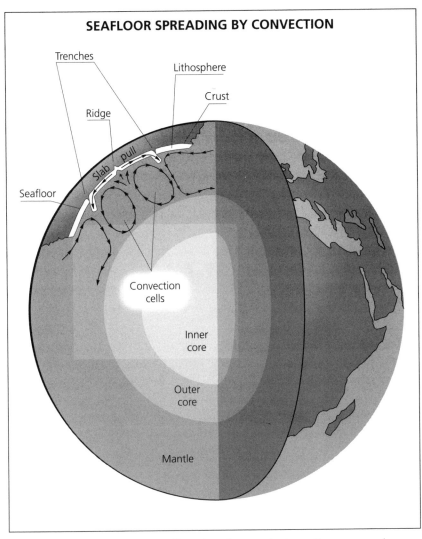

SEAFLOOR SPREADING BY CONVECTION

Trenches

Lithosphere

Crust

Ridge

Slab pull

Seafloor

Convection cells

Inner core

Outer core

Mantle

Hess believed that convection cells within the mantle drove the process of seafloor spreading.

In 1963 two young British geologists, Fred J. Vine and Drummond H. Matthews, and Lawrence Morley of the Canadian Geological Survey independently described magnetic anomalies that lent further evidence in support of seafloor spreading. Stripes parallel to the mid-oceanic ridge extended laterally from it, with reversals in the magnetic direction every several hundred kilometers. Vine thought that when the magma that erupted from the rift in the ridge cooled, it magnetized in the direction of the current magnetic field and then was carried

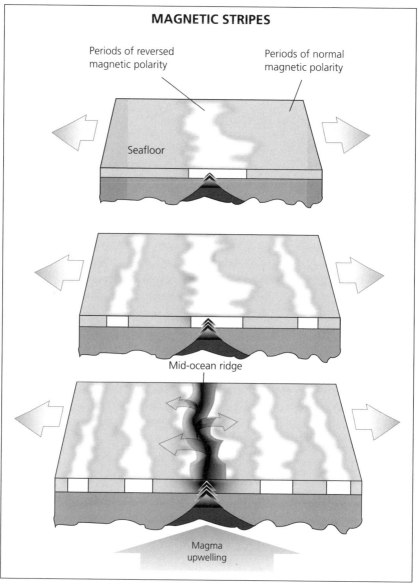

The zebra stripe magnetic pattern for the ocean floor provided supportive evidence for Hess's theory of seafloor spreading.

away laterally from the ridge. Hess wholeheartedly accepted this hypothesis. Further studies performed in 1966 on the magnetic stripes showed that the patterns were indeed parallel to the ridges and they were bilaterally symmetrical in magnetics and age. This evidence, along with evidence showing the seafloor was older the farther away it was from the ridges, confirmed the lateral movement of the crust and further established Hess's theory of seafloor spreading, as did future evidence of fossils and underwater core samples.

Admired and Honored

Beginning in 1962, Hess chaired the Space Science Advisory Board of the National Academy of Sciences. The board's responsibility was to advise NASA. In 1966 he was at Woods Hole, Massachusetts, chairing a meeting to discuss the scientific objectives of lunar exploration when he began having chest pains. He died of a heart attack on August 25, 1969, and was buried at the Arlington National Cemetery.

Hess was elected to membership of several academic societies, including the National Academy of Sciences (1952), the American Philosophical Society (1960), and the American Academy of Arts and Sciences (1968). He served as president of the Geodesy Section (1951–53) and the Tectonophysics Section (1956–58) of the American Geophysical Union, the Mineralogical Society of America (1955), and the Geological Society of America (1963). Because he was well respected as a scientist, he also was appointed chairman of the Committee for Disposal of Radioactive Wastes, chairman of the Earth Sciences Division of the National Research Council, and chairman of the Space Science Advisory Board of the National Academy of Sciences. Along with oceanographer Walter Munk, he was a principal player in the Mohole Project, the goal of which was to drill beneath the oceanic crust into the mantle. The Geological Society of America awarded Hess the Penrose Medal for distinguished achievement in the geological sciences in 1966, and NASA awarded Hess a Distinguished Public Service Award posthumously. The American Geophysical

Robert Sinclair Dietz

Robert Sinclair Dietz (September 14, 1914–May 19, 1995) was an American geologist who made contributions to a range of fields, including geology, marine geomorphology, and oceanography. He was interested in the structural changes that occurred over time to the continental terrace, slopes, and margins, the development of the Hawaiian swell, and meteorite craters. He also contributed to knowledge about the Arctic and Pacific basins.

Dietz received a bachelor's, master's, and doctorate degree, all in geology, from the University of Illinois. He performed most of his dissertation research at the Scripps Institution of Oceanography in San Diego with Francis P. Shepard. He studied *marine geology* and was one of the first to describe the underwater phosphorites off California.

Like Hess, Dietz was a military reservist called to active duty in 1941, after receiving his doctorate degree. After the war, he founded the Sea Floor Studies Section of the Naval Electronics Laboratory. He explored the geology of Antarctica, made bathymetry maps of the Arctic Ocean, and went on several oceanographic expeditions in the Pacific. In 1953 he became part of a venture called Geological Diving Consultants, which created seafloor geologic maps that were instrumental in the discovery of two major oil fields. Dietz became an accomplished *scuba* diver.

Union created the Harry H. Hess Medal for outstanding achievements in research in the constitution and evolution of the Earth and sister planets.

Hess's friends have described his personality as puckish and courageous. Part of Hess's greatness as a scientist was his willingness to entertain new ideas, even if they conflicted with his own previous conclusions. After all, sometimes wrong ideas ushered in new

On a Fulbright Scholarship, he studied underwater sound transmission at the University of Tokyo (1953) and then served with the Office of Naval Research (ONR) during the period 1954–58. He examined some of the same phenomena as Hess, including the unexpected discoveries regarding seafloor age and composition. In 1961 Dietz published a paper in *Nature* proposing essentially the same theory of seafloor spreading as Hess. Hess, however, already had issued preprints in 1960. Though Hess's official paper was not published until 1962, in 1963 Dietz publicly acknowledged Hess priority credit for the model of seafloor spreading.

While in London at ONR, Dietz met Belgian explorer Jacques Piccard, and together they convinced the world of the utility of the deep-sea submersible bathyscaphe for underwater exploration. Dietz and Piccard coauthored a book titled *Seven Miles Down: The Story of the Bathyscaphe TRIESTE* (1961), about the descent into the Challenger Deep in the Marianis Trench.

In 1963 Dietz started growing the oceanographic and geological studies group at the U.S. Coast and Geodetic Survey, which became the Environmental Sciences Administration, and then became part of the *National Oceanic and Atmospheric Administration* (NOAA). Working for the NOAA, he championed plate tectonics, the theory that was quickly evolving from the concept of seafloor spreading, a process he named. He retired from NOAA in 1975, accepted several visiting professorships around the United States, and landed a tenured professorship at Arizona State University in 1977. Dietz became an emeritus faculty in 1985 but continued researching until his death in 1995 in Tempe, Arizona.

eras of scientific accomplishment. In suggesting that the ocean basins were continuously recycled, Hess explained why seafloor spreading did not cause Earth to grow, why the layer of sediment on the ocean floor was thinner than expected, and why oceanic rocks are younger than continental rocks. Hess's model of seafloor spreading has become part of the foundation knowledge of the geological sciences and has evolved into the theory of plate tectonics.

Many questions regarding the forces that occur deep within the Earth are still actively being investigated today.

CHRONOLOGY

1906	Harry Hammond Hess is born on May 24 in New York City
1927	Receives a bachelor's degree in geology from Yale and starts field work in Africa
1929	Enrolls in graduate school at Princeton University
1931	Accompanies Dutch geophysicist Felix Andries Vening Meinesz on a submarine mission to measure gravity in West Indies and the Bahamas
1932	Receives a doctorate in geology from Princeton University and teaches at Rutgers
1933	Becomes a research associate at the Geophysical Laboratory of the Carnegie Institution
1934	Begins teaching at Princeton University
1941-45	Hess serves in the U.S. Navy during World War II. He creates bathymetric maps of the Pacific Ocean
1950-66	Chairs the geology department at Princeton University
1955	Serves as president of the Mineralogical Society of America
1960	Issues preprints of his revolutionary essay, "History of Ocean Basins," in which he proposes the model of seafloor spreading
1961	Attains the rank of rear admiral in the U.S. Navy
1962	Publishes "History of Ocean Basins" in *Petrologic Studies: A Volume in Honor of A. F. Buddington*
1963	Paleomagnetic evidence supports seafloor spreading
1966	The Geological Society of America awards Hess the Penrose Medal for distinguished achievement in the geological sciences
1969	Dies on August 25 at Woods Hole, Massachusetts

FURTHER READING

Biographical Memoirs. Vol. 43. New York: Columbia University Press, 1973. Memoir of Hess, written by a distinguished colleague for the premier scientific organization of the United States.

Carruthers, Margaret W., and Susan Clinton. *Pioneers of Geology: Discovering Earth's Secrets.* New York: Franklin Watts, 2001. Includes a chapter on Hess that outlines the evolution of his concept of seafloor spreading.

Holmes, Frederic L., ed. *Dictionary of Scientific Biography.* Vol. 17, Supplement II. New York: Scribner, 1990. Good source for facts concerning personal backgrounds and scientific accomplishments but assumes reader has basic knowledge of science.

Kious, W. Jacqueline, and Robert I. Tilling. *This Dynamic Earth: The Story of Plate Tectonics.* U.S. Geological Survey. Available online. URL: http://pubs.usgs.gov/publications/text/dynamic.html. Last updated on September 29, 2003. Originally published in paper form in 1996, this site is full of information regarding plate tectonics. Includes several helpful diagrams and a biographical profile of Hess under "Developing the theory."

Simonis, Doris A., ed. *Lives and Legacies: Scientists, Mathematicians, and Inventors.* Phoenix, Ariz.: Oryx Press, 1999. Contains one-page profiles.

7

Jacques-Yves Cousteau

(1910–1997)

Jacques-Yves Cousteau brought the wonders of the sea to television and lured people into the ocean through his development of scuba. *(Poerterfield-Chickering/Photo Researchers, Inc.)*

The Invention of the Aqualung and Popularization of Marine Biology

Colorful images of the undersea world flood cable television, animated films feature life on the ocean floor, and millions of people dive as a hobby. As few as 50 years ago, people were unaware of what life was like under the sea; biologists had barely identified a fraction of the many varied marine life-forms, much less studied their habits and ecosystems. Yet man has always been intrigued by the mysterious depths of the ocean.

The first diving bell was patented in 1690 by Edmund Halley (for whom Halley's Comet is named), and it allowed men to remain submerged for up to 90 minutes. In the 1800s, clever inventors devised apparatuses consisting of hoses that pumped air into diving suits, giving divers slightly more freedom of movement than a diving bell. American naturalist William Beebe descended to a record 3,028 feet (923 m) in a globe-shaped bathysphere and observed fantastical sites in 1934, whetting the appetite of marine scientists. A decade later, French pioneer oceanographer Jacques-Yves Cousteau launched a new era in marine exploration and opened up the undersea world to amateur divers through his invention of the aqualung, today called scuba (*s*elf-*c*ontained *u*nderwater *b*reathing *a*pparatus). His advancements in underwater photography brought the indescribable marvels of the ocean deeps into living rooms around the world, inspiring future oceanographers to explore what he called a "world without sun."

A Childhood on the Move

Elizabeth Duranthon Cousteau gave birth to Jacques-Yves Cousteau on June 11, 1910, in the small coastal town of Saint-André-de-Cubzac, near the Bordeaux region in France. Jacques's father, Daniel, was a lawyer who worked as a personal secretary for a wealthy American businessman. His occupation required frequent travel between Paris, France, and New York City in the United States, and the Cousteau family accompanied him. Jacques learned to swim when he was only four years old, but because he was a sickly child who suffered from chronic enteritis, (inflammation of the intestines), he was not allowed to physically exert himself very often. His mother worried about the possible negative effects of too much traveling, so in 1917 she enrolled Jacques and his older brother Pierre at a French boarding school. His health was still frail, but he passed his classes. When his father's employer suggested that more exercise, specifically swimming, would increase Jacques's strength, the course of his future was established.

Jacques became a very strong swimmer and spent his 10th summer at a camp in Vermont where one of the campers' duties was to clean up dead branches and debris from the bottom of the lake. As a teenager he enjoyed tinkering with models and machines and took them apart for the challenge of reassembling them. Having developed an interest in moviemaking, he purchased a movie camera that he took with him everywhere. Jacques was bored at school and began causing trouble. After he smashed 17 school windows, the headmaster expelled him, and his parents sent him to a very strict boarding school in Ribeauvillé. The discipline at the military-like school corrected his behavior, and his grades improved. He graduated with honors at age 19 but did not care to continue his education.

In 1930 Cousteau passed a competitive entrance examination for the French Naval Academy at Brest. After he graduated second in his class with a degree in engineering, Cousteau joined the French Navy and was assigned to a cruiser in the Far East from 1933 to 1935. Afterward, he returned home and decided he wanted to fly, so he enrolled in a year-long naval aviation course.

Career-Changing Accident

One day in 1936, Cousteau borrowed his father's sports car to attend a friend's wedding in the Vosges Mountains. While speeding around the mountain curves, he hit a guard rail and was severely injured. He was in and out of consciousness for several days, only to wake up and learn that his left arm was broken in five places and his right arm was paralyzed and grossly infected. The doctors recommended amputation, but Cousteau adamantly refused and suffered through a long, painful recovery. Swimming helped restore his strength. Though he eventually rehabilitated both arms, his right arm remained slightly twisted for the rest of his life. By the end of 1936 he was ready for active duty, but his disability prevented him from flying. The navy assigned him to a position as an artillery instructor at the base in Toulon, along the Mediterranean coast.

The following year he married Simone Melchoir, with whom he had two sons, Jean-Michel in 1938 and Philippe in 1940. They bought a home on the shores of Sanary, not far from the Toulon base. Simone's father had been in the navy, and she shared Cousteau's interest in the sea. She became an accomplished diver herself and later accompanied him on almost all of his expeditions. They were married until Simone's death in 1990.

At Toulon, Cousteau befriended two other men who loved swimming as much as he did, Lieutenant Philippe Taillez and Frédéric Dumas. Though Cousteau was able to dive deeper than most—he could dive 60 feet (about 18 m)—he wondered how man could stay underwater longer than one full breath would permit. The atmosphere contains 21 percent oxygen, 78 percent nitrogen, and 1 percent other substances. Previous divers had attempted using tanks filled with compressed oxygen, but at great depths oxygen became toxic. Despite this knowledge, Cousteau started experimenting with a gas mask, inner tubes, and an oxygen bottle, but after breathing the compressed oxygen underwater for only four minutes, he suffered a seizure. He tinkered with his equipment some more, and tried again, only to suffer another seizure. This experience convinced Cousteau that compressed air was a better choice.

Cousteau sought advice from his father-in-law, Henri Melchoir, an executive for Air Liquide, a company that sold gases. They discussed the potential utility of a self-regulating valve that could control the release of compressed air and allow a diver to inhale and exhale through the same mechanism without contaminating the fresh air. Cousteau's investigations into this matter were delayed when France and Great Britain declared war on Germany in September 1939, and he became a gunnery officer on a naval cruiser, the *Dupliex*, that was stationed at the Toulon port in the Mediterranean. His shipmates appreciated his diving skills when a steel cable became tangled in the shaft and propeller, and Cousteau and five other volunteers dived down and back until they freed the cable. The task was exhausting and convinced Cousteau of the need to develop an underwater breathing apparatus.

Invention of the Aqualung

A breakthrough occurred in December of 1942, when Melchoir arranged for Cousteau to meet with Émile Gagnan, an engineer for Air Liquide. Gagnan had a self-regulating valve similar to the one Cousteau desired. Together they modified it and then tested it with a tank of compressed air in the Marne River outside Paris. To their dismay, their prototype only worked when the diver was horizontal. Within a few weeks, however, they had successfully adjusted their device, which they named an aqualung, and applied for a patent.

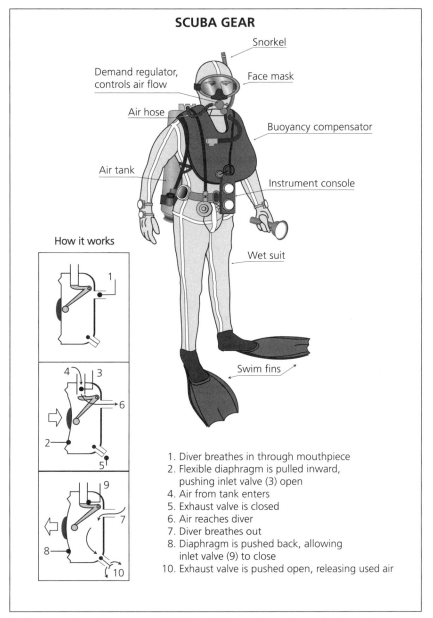

SCUBA GEAR

Snorkel

Demand regulator, controls air flow

Face mask

Air hose

Buoyancy compensator

Air tank

Instrument console

How it works

Wet suit

Swim fins

1. Diver breathes in through mouthpiece
2. Flexible diaphragm is pulled inward, pushing inlet valve (3) open
4. Air from tank enters
5. Exhaust valve is closed
6. Air reaches diver
7. Diver breathes out
8. Diaphragm is pushed back, allowing inlet valve (9) to close
10. Exhaust valve is pushed open, releasing used air

Scuba gear gives divers unrestricted mobility underwater and allows them to remain submerged for extended periods of time.

The aqualung weighed 50 pounds (22.7 kg) but was not burdensome underwater and allowed the diver to swim freely. Cousteau, Taillez, and Dumas established limits for safe diving and experimented with mixtures of different gases and ascension rates. They dove hundreds of times and were delighted by what they saw underwater. Cousteau wanted to capture the hidden beauty on film and show it to the world. He built a watertight case around his camera, spliced together still-camera film (since movie film was scarce during the war), and used a clothespin to adjust the lens inside the casing. The result, his first underwater film, *Eighteen Meters Down*, won praises at the Cannes Film Festival in 1943. One scene ironically portrayed Dumas calmly feeding fish, the life-form upon which he normally fed.

Cousteau improved his equipment to withstand deeper dives, and several films followed. In 1943 he filmed divers wearing aqualungs swimming among fishes while exploring sunken ships. Adequate lighting posed a unique problem, as light could not penetrate far through the water. Cousteau had only observed dark greens and dull grays at depths of 50–100 feet (approximately 15–30 m) previously, but when he brought plant and *algae* specimens from the depths to the surface, he was surprised to see all sorts of brilliant oranges and flamboyant reds. He soon experimented with artificial lighting and color film.

Undersea Research Group

Cousteau worked as a spy for the French Resistance during World War II and was decorated with the Legion of Honor, France's highest military honor. After the war, the navy assigned Cousteau to a desk job. Taillez became a forest ranger, and Dumas, a civilian, was the only one of the three close friends who was able to continue living at the beach. To get back in the water, Cousteau convinced the authorities of the need for a formal Undersea Research Group. Taillez served as the group's commandant, since he ranked the highest, and Dumas was recruited as a civilian specialist. The three were happy to be diving together again in Toulon, even though their missions were quite dangerous. They were responsible for clearing debris from the port and for finding and disarming German mines. They also made a short movie that showed the general public how a submarine laid mines. Audiences

Diving Dangers

As a diver descends, pressure increases due to the weight of the water above him. If a diver remains submerged for a long period of time, a condition called *decompression sickness,* or the *bends,* might result. Gases, especially nitrogen, build up in the body's tissues as the increased pressure forces them into the liquid state. Rapid ascent causes an abrupt decrease in the pressure surrounding the body, leading to the formation of gas bubbles in the body's tissues. As dissolved gases come out of solution, bubbles in the body's tissues may cause pain, itchiness, blindness, dizziness, paralysis, and even death.

A diver can avoid the symptoms of decompression sickness by ascending slowly, in a stepwise manner. Halting for a few minutes every few feet will allow the pressure between the air in the lungs and the water to equalize. This prevents bubbles from forming when the air attempts to expand as the pressure decreases. A slow ascent gives the diver time to exhale the excess nitrogen that may have accumulated during a dive.

Nitrogen narcosis is a condition that most often results at extreme depths from the accumulation of excess nitrogen in the body's tissues. The diver feels drugged and loses his ability to reason. Inhalation of a gaseous mixture containing helium in place of nitrogen helps prevent nitrogen narcosis. Breathing pure oxygen at extreme depths is also very dangerous and may cause nausea, dizziness, and seizures.

were stunned to witness a torpedo (unarmed) gliding through the water past the camera.

The reputation of the Underwater Research Group grew, and the men were asked to explore the phenomenon of the Fountain of Vaucluse, near Avignon. Every spring the fountain erupted into a raging flood for five weeks. Cousteau and Dumas confirmed that the fountain originated from a flooded underground cavern system. While exploring the caves, Cousteau recognized symptoms of what he believed to be nitrogen narcosis, a condition that occurs at extreme depths and causes a diver to lose his ability to reason. The men unwisely continued their exploration until Dumas lost consciousness. After a difficult struggle, Cousteau dragged Dumas to the surface, where he was resuscitated and recovered. Analysis of the air left in the cylinders demonstrated higher than normal levels of carbon monoxide in the air. Further investigation revealed that the new diesel-powered air compressor had been sucking in its own exhaust and filling the tanks with the fumes. This experience reminded Cousteau that safety was an ever-present concern.

Aware of the threat of nitrogen narcosis, Cousteau wondered how deep humans could dive safely. To explore the limits, his team assembled an apparatus for measuring the depth a diver reached by attaching boards along the length of a weighted rope. As he passed a certain depth, a diver would sign his name to the deepest board he could reach, and when the rope was pulled up, the team could measure the depth the diver had reached. While in the water, divers constantly tugged at the rope to signal they were okay. Cousteau himself successfully reached 297 feet (90.5 m) in 1947. One day, the signals of a fellow accomplished diver, Maurice Fargues, stopped. Others immediately dove in to retrieve him and found his lifeless body at 150 feet (45.7 m). He had succumbed to decompression sickness while ascending after signing the board at 396 feet (120.7 m). Cousteau became even more worried about safety and set 300 feet (91.4 m) as the absolute limit.

The *Calypso*

Around this same time, Swiss physicist Auguste Piccard was preparing for the maiden voyage on his newly developed bathyscaph. The bathyscaph, a thick steel spherical craft attached to a hull and used for deep-sea observation, descended to a depth of 4,600 feet (1,400 m). Cousteau was anxious to have his own sea-faring vehicle and convinced a wealthy British philanthropist to finance the purchase and refitting of a former minesweeper into an ocean exploration vessel. The 151-foot (46-m) long *Calypso* was equipped with a high observation deck, an underwater viewing chamber, and a diving well that penetrated the ship's hull.

After hiring specialists in geology, hydrology, and biology, Captain Cousteau and the *Calypso* set off on an expedition of the Red Sea on November 24, 1951. The crew visited and explored coral reefs and islands, discovered volcanic basins on the seafloor, identified rare plants and animals, collected specimens of many new species, and charted a new record depth of 16,500 feet (5,030 m). Cousteau filmed everything and continued to be amazed at the abundant life and vibrant colors that decorated the undersea world. His films astonished scientists and amateur naturalists, but most importantly, impressed the National Geographic Society (NGS), the world's largest nonprofit scientific and educational organization, which offered to finance a future expedition.

During the summer of 1952, Cousteau explored a shipwreck off the island of Grand Congloué, southeast of Marseilles. From the examination of artifacts brought to the surface from 164 feet (50 m) by Cousteau and his divers, archaeologists estimated the ship to be over 2,200 years old. The Roman ship still contained many unbroken, sealed jars of wine, one from which Cousteau tasted a sample. Investigators hypothesized that the ship had been on the way to Marseilles to sell the wine when it crashed into the island and sunk. A thorough excavation took five years, and archeologists, anthropologists, and other scientists were thrilled to see the filmed underwater artifacts that offered a rare glimpse into the buried past. The *Calypso* diving crew also was the first to conduct offshore oil surveys.

Cousteau published *The Silent World* with Frédéric Dumas in 1953. The 266-page illustrated, instantly successful, best-selling book chronicled his early dives and explorations of underwater caves and shipwrecks. Cousteau believed the adventurous theme was worthy of a full-length documentary, which he produced and codirected with Louis Malle. The film shared the book's title and debuted at the Cannes Film Festival in 1956, winning the festival's highest award, and the following year, an Oscar award for best documentary. Cousteau went on to produce over 70 full-length films and television specials, many award-winning, covering his expeditions aboard the *Calypso*.

In 1957 Cousteau resigned from the navy. Despite his Resistance medal and impressive minesweeping work, as a captain, he was ranked lower than most of his former classmates, and he wanted to devote more time to ocean exploration. Prince Rainier of Monaco asked Cousteau to serve as director of the Oceanographic Institute of Monaco, a position that permitted Cousteau to continue conducting his own business aboard the *Calypso*. In 1959 he built his own two-man diving saucer that could descend to 1,146 feet (350 m) and remain submerged for six hours. Using this small submarine, he was able to examine the layers of oceanic life at various levels for extended periods of time.

The Conshelf Experiments

Cousteau wondered if man could ever live on the ocean floor. To explore this possibility, in 1962 he built a living chamber on a *continental shelf*, a shallow underwater plain bordering a continent. Called Conshelf, the watertight chamber was situated approximately 39 feet (12 m) below the surface of the Mediterranean Sea near Marseilles. Radio and video cables provided a connection between the surface and the living quarters for two *aquanauts*. The aquanauts left the chamber daily to explore the surrounding oceanic waters and hosted visitors. After one week, they exhibited no negative physiological effects.

The following year, Cousteau arranged for Conshelf II to be anchored in the Red Sea northeast of Port Sudan. The station was slightly larger and contained two chambers: Starfish House located at 33 feet (10 m) deep and Deep Cabin located at 98 feet (30 m). Five aquanauts lived in Starfish House for four weeks, and two aquanauts lived in Deep Cabin for one week. Cousteau believed that a helium-rich atmosphere would allow the divers to go deeper, thus the Deep Cabin was filled with half air and half helium gas.

Cousteau's development of underwater photographic techniques gave the world a diver's view of unique oceanic life-forms. *(Courtesy of OAR/National Undersea Research Program)*

The divers were able to dive to 360 feet (110 m) safely, proving Cousteau correct. Cousteau produced a film called *World Without Sun* that detailed life in the Conshelf II. The film won an Oscar award in 1964 for best documentary.

In September of 1965, a third Conshelf station was set up at 354 feet (108 m) in the Mediterranean Sea. Six men lived in the globe-shaped chamber for 28 days. The Conshelf experiments proved that man could live underwater without suffering negative physiological effects. The cost was too prohibitive to pursue this further, however, and the unattractive squeaky voices of the aquanauts that resulted from helium inhalation prevented Cousteau from finding a distributor. Cousteau's dream of establishing permanent underwater homes and oceanic workshops by the 21st century would never be realized.

Legacy of Conservation

Cousteau devoted the remainder of his career to producing film series and television specials, including *The Undersea World of Jacques Cousteau*, *Cousteau Odyssey*, and *Cousteau Amazon*. Viewers continued to be fascinated by his straightforward yet intriguing films about ocean exploration, and his documentaries received over 40 Emmy nominations. Cousteau authored dozens of books, including two of his most popular, *The Living Sea* (1963) and *The Ocean World* (1985). He also published a 20-volume encyclopedia, *The Ocean World of Jacques Cousteau* (1973–74).

Cousteau used his fame to promote a message of conservation and protection of the world's oceans. As a source for food, minerals, and rainfall, as well as being a temperature moderator, the oceans were too valuable to pollute or exploit. He founded the nonprofit Cousteau Society in 1973 to communicate this message. He showed the public photographs of marine organisms tangled in nets and ocean debris to garner support. In 1991 he started a petition to adopt a "Bill of Rights for Future Generations" that addressed the long-range troubles caused by pollution. He was appointed to the United Nations High Level Advisory Board on Sustainable Development in 1993. France named Cousteau chairman of a newly created Council on the Rights of Future

Generations, but Cousteau resigned in 1995 to protest nuclear testing in the Pacific Ocean.

Simone, Cousteau's wife of over 50 years, died in 1990. Cousteau married Francine Triplet the following year. They already had two children together, Diane, born in 1980, and Pierre-Yves in 1982.

In 1996 the *Calypso* was struck by a barge in Singapore. Though he wanted to repair it and build a second research vessel, Cousteau was suffering from a respiratory ailment that caused him to be hospitalized for several months. The world's most famous underwater explorer died from heart failure, in Paris, on June 15, 1997, at 87 years of age.

Cousteau had received several honorary degrees from universities, including Harvard and the University of California at Berkeley. He was a member of the French Academy of Sciences and a foreign member of the prominent National Academy of Sciences. He was also awarded the NGS's gold medal in 1961, the International Environmental Prize of the United Nations in 1977, and the U.S. Presidential Medal of Freedom in 1985. He was inducted into the National Wildlife Federation Conservation Hall of Fame in 2000.

The invention of the aqualung allowed divers to breathe comfortably while freely exploring the previously inaccessible ocean world. This equipment opened the ocean floor to marine scientists and led to the discovery of new intricate ecosystems found in the deep sea. Being reasonably affordable and relatively easy to learn how to use, millions have adopted scuba diving as a hobby. Cousteau's advancement of underwater photographic techniques and his production of breathtaking films on marine life popularized marine biology and prepared general audiences for hearing and accepting the important message of preservation of the world's oceans.

CHRONOLOGY

1910	Jacques Cousteau is born on June 11 in Saint-André-de-Cubzac, France
1930–33	Attends the French Naval Academy, earning a degree in engineering

1933	Joins French navy
1943	Invents aqualung with French engineer Émile Gagnan and produces first professional film, *Eighteen Meters Down*
1945	The Underwater Research Group is formed
1951	The *Calypso* embarks on its first voyage, an expedition to the Red Sea
1953	Publishes his first book, *The Silent World*, which he later develops into a film
1957	Resigns from the French Navy and becomes director of the Oceanographic Institute of Monaco
1962–65	Conducts Conshelf experiments to explore the possibility of human underwater habitation
1964	Produces the film *World without Sun*
1968	The television program *Undersea World of Jacques Cousteau* airs, lasting for eight years
1974	Founds the Cousteau Society to educate people about the Earth's water systems
1997	Dies of respiratory disease on June 15 at age 87

FURTHER READING

The Cousteau Society. Available online: URL: http://www. cousteau.org. Accessed on January 18, 2005. The Web site of the society founded by Cousteau. Follow links through "Heritage" to find information on the man, his achievements, the *Calypso*, and pictures.

DuTemple, Lesley A. *Jacques Cousteau*. Minneapolis, Minn.: Lerner Publications Company, 2000. Written for young adults, easy to read, complete biography with a time line and additional resources listed.

King, Roger. *Jacques Cousteau and the Undersea World*. Philadelphia, Pa.: Chelsea House Publishers, 2001. Describes Cousteau's inventions and investigations as well as his impact on marine exploration. Appropriate for young adults.

Markham, Lois. *Jacques-Yves Cousteau: Exploring the Wonders of the Deep.* Austin, Tex.: Raintree Steck-Vaughn Publishers, 1997. Examines the early influences and reveals the discoveries of the famous French marine explorer.

Munson, Richard. *Cousteau: The Captain and His World.* New York: William Morrow and Company, 1989. An unauthorized biography of Cousteau written for adults.

Scientists and Inventors. New York: Macmillan Library Reference, 1998. Brief profiles of the lives and works of over 100 notable scientists, written for juvenile readers.

Eugenie Clark

8

(1922–   )

Eugenie Clark is an expert ichthyologist and a pioneer in the study of shark behavior. *(Courtesy of Ruth Petzold)*

Expert on Poisonous Fish and Shark Behavior

In Queens, New York, a young girl read about naturalist William Beebe's dives into the deep abyss of the ocean while inside a bathysphere. His descriptions of the mysterious and fascinating lifeforms intrigued her, as she was a fish lover herself. When she declared her goal was to become an explorer of marine life just like Beebe, her mother responded that someday she might become a secretary for someone like him. The determined girl, Eugenie Clark, went on to become a famous ichthyologist (one who studies fish) and a world-renowned expert on sharks.

An Early Fascination with Fish

Eugenie Clark was born on May 4, 1922, in New York, New York, to Charles and Yumiko Clark. Her mother was a swim instructor, and her father was the manager of a private pool. He died when Genie was only two years old, and by then, she already knew how to swim. They lived with Genie's Japanese grandmother in Queens but often went to the beach on Long Island where they used chewing gum to plug their ears before plunging into the ocean. Her mother worked to support the family at a newspaper and cigar stand in the lobby of the Downtown Athletic Club. Genie often accompanied her on Saturdays and waited for lunchtime at the nearby New York Aquarium, where she amused herself by watching the fish swim swiftly and gracefully in their long tanks. She soon began collecting fish at home in a 15-gallon (57-liter) tank, became the youngest member accepted into the Queens County Aquarium Society, and learned to keep methodical records of all her pets. By the time she entered high school, she also kept pet snakes, toads, salamanders, and alligators, and biology was her favorite subject.

After graduation Genie enrolled at Hunter College in New York City with plans to major in zoology. In addition to taking every zoology course offered, she took field courses in zoology and botany at the University of Michigan Biological Station during the summers. After obtaining a bachelor's degree in 1942, she worked as a chemist for the Celanese Corporation of America at their plastics research labs in New Jersey. In 1942 Clark married a pilot named Hideo "Roy" Umaki, but during their marriage they did not spend much time together. He served in the army and was stationed overseas. They divorced in 1949.

Clark entered graduate school at New York University (NYU) to study zoology, and more specifically, ichthyology. She researched the puffing mechanism of blowfish (the order *Tetraodontiformes* or *Plectognathi* includes the triggerfishes, puffers, filefishes, boxfishes, globefishes, and ocean sunfishes) under the guidance of Dr. Charles Breder, who was the curator of the department of fishes and taught an ichthyology class at the American Museum of Natural History. He was so impressed with her work that he published her research results in the museum's scientific magazine, *Bulletin of the American Museum of Natural History*, "A Contribution to the Visceral Anatomy Development, and Relationships of the Plectognathi" (1947).

Clark met Dr. Carl Hubbs, from the Scripps Institution of Oceanography of the University of California, at the 1945 meeting of the American Society of Ichthyologists and Herpetologists in Pittsburgh, Pennsylvania. When she completed her master's degree in zoology from NYU in 1946, she joined him as a part-time research assistant and began research toward a doctorate degree. Hubbs taught Clark to dive with a face mask and to walk on the ocean floor using a metal helmet connected by a long hose to a compressed air supply aboard a ship. Scuba gear was not yet widely available.

Respected Ichthyologist

In 1947 the U.S. Fish and Wildlife Service hired Clark to study fish in the waters surrounding the Philippines, but en route she was delayed in Hawaii only to learn that they had changed their mind due to her gender. Though disappointed, Clark used her time in Hawaii to explore the waters around the islands and study tiny tropical puffers. She returned to NYU and continued her dissertation studies on the mating habits of platies and swordtails under the supervision of Professor Myron Gordon. In aquariums, platies and swordfishes mated to create hybrid fish, but hybrids were never found in the wild. Clark described the act of true copulation in platies and determined that in a competition between sperm of the two different species, the same-species sperm had an advantage over sperm from a different species. This meant that even if both species deposited sperm inside a female, the sperm from the same species as the female would successfully fertilize the eggs. Clark also performed the first successful artificial insemination of a fish in the United States.

While working toward a Ph.D. in zoology, in 1949 Clark accepted a job studying the fish of the South Seas for the Scientific Investigation in Micronesia program of the U.S. Office of Naval Research. Since the United States had acquired many of the South Pacific Islands after World War II, the navy wanted to know if commercial fishing in the area would be profitable and which fish were safe to eat and which were poisonous. One method Clark used for collecting fish was to add rotenone to tide pools. Rotenone is a chemical that can be extracted from plant roots that stuns the fish, causing them to float to the surface. The fish are still safe for consumption, and the vegetation is not harmed. Clark caught many interesting specimens, some of which were normally hidden or too small to be captured by other methods. She preserved the specimens in formalin and then shipped them to the American Museum of Natural History in alcohol. From the islands of Micronesia, Guam, Kwajalein, and Palau, Clark collected hundreds of specimens from the tide pools and also several puffers that she sent back to California for poison analysis. On the Palauan island of Koror, a skilled spearfisherman named Siakong taught Clark to hold her breath for a long time underwater and to spearfish near the coral reefs. She found many new types of plectognaths and other fish she had never seen before and encountered sharks and razor-toothed barracudas. Meeting the natives and experiencing their cultures was as enjoyable for Clark as exploring the rich marine flora and fauna of the region.

In 1950 Clark married a charming, young Greek orthopedic surgeon named Ilias Papakonstantinou (later shortened to Konstantinou). They had two daughters and two sons during the next seven years.

Clark earned a doctorate in zoology from NYU in 1950 and received a Fulbright Scholarship to study fish of the Red Sea in the Middle East. The Red Sea is very warm and salty, and its name comes from the reddish appearance caused by tiny red algae that live on its surface. Clark had read an article describing the *commensal* relationship between a sea anemone and a clown fish and found many similarities between the Red Sea and the tropical Pacific Ocean. She also remembered that many of the tropical plectognaths she studied had been described originally by ichthyologists from the Red Sea. Surprisingly, no one had scientifically analyzed the Red Sea fish in 70 years. Using the Marine Biological Station in Ghardaqa, Egypt, as a base, she traveled around, collected specimens of over 300 species, wrote detailed descriptions, discovered three new

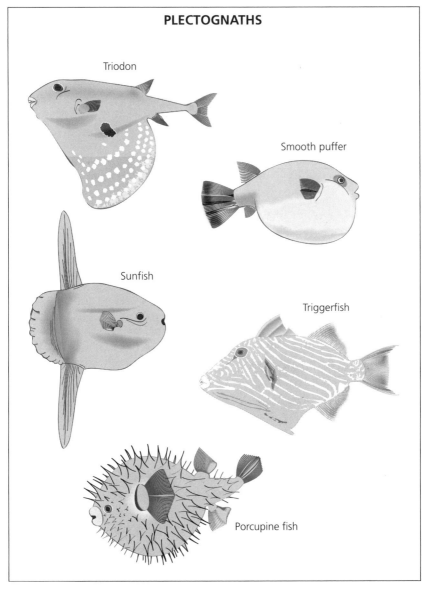

PLECTOGNATHS

Triodon

Smooth puffer

Sunfish

Triggerfish

Porcupine fish

Throughout her career, Clark has studied many types of plectognaths, which include a wide variety of unusual fish such as puffers.

species, and performed dissections of the many forms of marine life. The only poisonous fish she found were puffers. Several scientific papers and a best-selling autobiography, *Lady with a Spear* (1953), resulted from her year spent exploring the Red Sea.

Back in New York, Clark taught biology at Hunter College and conducted ichthyological research at the American Museum of Natural History. She also lectured at educational institutions around the country.

A Lab of Her Own

One reader of Clark's autobiography happened to be a wealthy Floridian with a son who was interested in marine biology. Anne Vanderbilt and her husband William invited Clark to their home on the Cape Haze peninsula. The meeting began a long association between Clark and the Vanderbilts, who funded the Cape Haze Marine Laboratory for her to direct in Placida, Florida, right on the Gulf of Mexico. The lab opened in 1955.

The first marine mystery Clark solved at her new lab was regarding a fish called the belted sand bass from the genus *Serranus*. She observed several egg-carrying fish and assumed they were females, but she could not locate any of the males. Dissection and microscopic examination revealed not only eggs, but also sperm. The fish were *hermaphroditic*, meaning they had the reproductive organs of both males and females. The fish could switch from male to female in less than 10 seconds, and their coloring changed at the same time. They could even fertilize their own eggs.

Prompted by a request for fresh shark livers by Dr. John Heller, a medical researcher from the New England Institute of Medicine, Clark broadened her focus from fish reproduction to sharks. She identified 18 species living off the coast, including hammerhead, blackfin, dog fish, nurse, tiger, bull, lemon, and sandbar sharks. She performed hundreds of dissections and examined their stomach contents to learn about their diet, finding mostly small fish, crabs, eels, octopuses, and other sharks. She built pens at the end of the dock so she could keep live sharks for observation. Dr. Perry Gilbert, a shark expert from Cornell University, taught Clark to spray a chemical at the mouth and over the gills of sharks to render

Nurse shark. Clark's research dispelled the myth that all sharks are ferocious man-eaters. *(Courtesy of Florida Keys National Marine Sanctuary)*

them unconscious for about 10 minutes, during which time the workers could haul the sharks safely into the pens. Over the 12 years that Clark directed the Cape Haze Marine Laboratory (which moved to Sarasota in the early 1960s), Clark became an expert on sharks and earned the nickname "Shark Lady." The National Science Foundation and the Office of Naval Research provided financial assistance in the form of grants that Clark used to expand the lab, build more shark pens, and execute research.

Shark Behavior

Though many people believed sharks were dangerous and stupid creatures, no one ever had investigated their behavior. After observing lemon sharks swimming toward people approaching their tanks as if they expected to be fed, Clark believed they were capable of learning. To teach a shark to associate a ringing bell with food, she painted a square wooden target white, hung fish from it, and lowered it by rope into the shark pen. When the shark went for the bait, he bumped into the target, and a bell sounded. After three days, she lowered the fish only after the shark bumped the target rather than have it attached, then progressively lowered the fish farther and farther away from the target until the shark had to

Sharks

Sharks (class: Chondrichthyes, subclass: Elasmobranchii) first appeared over 400 million years ago, even before the dinosaurs. Over 370 species are known. They live in every ocean, and even some rivers and lakes. As cartilaginous fish, they do not have bony skeletons, and instead of a gas-filled swim bladder, they have a large, oil-rich liver that keeps them buoyant. Sharks range in size from six inches (15 cm) to 50 feet (15 m) in length. Their bodies are streamlined for swimming, which they do even when sleeping. As they glide through the water, water flows through their mouths and over their gills so oxygen can be taken into the shark's blood circulation. Sharks have several rows of teeth that are con-

swim to the other side of the pen to retrieve his food. Clark also performed experiments showing that sharks can distinguish colors and shapes. Her research demonstrated that sharks were actually intelligent creatures with the ability to learn and remember.

When Akihito, future emperor of Japan, who was interested in ichthyology and had studied many types of fish, invited Clark as his guest in 1965, she brought him a nurse shark that she had trained to ask for food by bumping a target. She was surprised to learn that he had never gone diving, so a few years later, in 1967, when he stopped by Sarasota on the way from South America back to Japan, Clark met him at 5:30 A.M., before any reporters were around, and taught him to skin dive.

New York and Maryland

Though sharks were the main thrust of her research, Clark also engaged in other scientific activities. Exploration of nearby freshwater springs led to the discovery of many ancient human bones and stantly replaced. They may have up to 3,000 at one time and over a life-time shed thousands. Their excellent hearing, sight, and smell make them competent predators.

One of Eugenie Clark's self-proclaimed, most important accomplishments was dispelling some of the falsehoods regarding sharks. Propelled by the media's fantastical accounts of shark attacks on beaches and Hollywood's depictions in films, sharks have developed a reputation of being ferocious manhunters. According to the International Shark Attack File (administered by the American Elasmobranch Society and the Florida Museum of Natural History), in 2003 there were only 55 unprovoked attacks by sharks on humans. Often times the shark mistakes the swimmer for fish, a marine mammal, or other natural prey. Sharks, on the other hand, are particularly vulnerable to overfishing by humans since they take a long time to mature and only have a few young.

other traces of Native American life from over 7,000 years ago. In 1959 Clark broke the record for the deepest dive with compressed air for a woman at 210 feet (64 m). During a trip with her family to the Middle East sponsored by the National Geographic Society (NGS) in 1964, she investigated a colony of garden eels near Elat, Israel, and identified and named new species of sandfish found in the Red Sea *Trichonotous nikii* (after her youngest son Niki).

Clark divorced Konstantinou and married a writer named Chandler Brossard in 1967. They moved back to New York with her four children, but a few years later the children returned to Florida because they missed the weather and the waters of the Gulf of Mexico. When she left the laboratory, she recommended Perry Gilbert from Cornell to succeed her as director. With financial assistance from a businessman named William Mote, the lab was expanded and renamed the Mote Marine Laboratory. Today scientists continue to research a variety of marine disciplines at the laboratory, which consists of research centers to study sharks, marine mammals, and sea turtles, fisheries enhancement, eco-toxicology, coastal ecology, aquaculture research and development, and tropical research (located in Summerland Key). Mote also offers a series of educational programs, houses aquarium exhibits, and runs a dolphin and whale hospital.

For two years, Clark taught zoology at the City College of New York and was a visiting professor at the New England Institute for Medical Research. Then she accepted a position in the zoology department at the University of Maryland in 1968 and was promoted to full professor in 1973. In 1969 she published a second autobiography titled *The Lady and the Sharks*. Many of her discoveries were published in over a dozen articles that she wrote for *National Geographic* magazine. The marriage between Clark and Brossard dissolved, and in 1970 Clark married a scientist from the National Institutes of Health named Igor Klatzo. That marriage also ended in divorce.

Shark Repellent and Sleeping Sharks

In 1972 Clark examined fluid secreted by the Moses sole, a sand-dwelling flat fish that she had first observed a dozen years before. The whitish substance that oozed from pores by the fins made her fingers tingly and numb and killed sea urchins and reef fishes in small doses. When she placed a Moses sole in a shark tank as bait, the mouths of sharks seemed to freeze open as they approached the fish, and the sharks wildly shook their heads back and forth. When she put one on an 80-foot (24-m) line with nine other types of fish and lowered it into the sea, sharks consumed all the fish except the Moses sole. She brought it up and rubbed the scales with alcohol then lowered it again, and it was immediately eaten. Putting a small shark in a tank with the fluid killed the shark in six hours. She wondered if the Moses sole produced a substance that could act as a shark repellent. Though initial studies seemed promising, the substance was unstable at room temperature and could not be sold for general use. As Clark learned more about sharks, she did not believe shark repellents were necessary anyhow; people were more dangerous to sharks than sharks were to people. She felt that understanding the creatures' behavior and acting accordingly was a better measure against shark attacks. The Moses sole also produced an antidote for its own poison that was later found to protect against bee, scorpion, and snake venom, but the antidote had to be injected at the same time as the poison itself to be effective.

A friend in Mexico sent Clark photographs of sharks in underwater caves off the Yucatán Peninsula and described some unusual behavior. The sharks seemed to be sleeping or dazed. Clark was interested and, in 1975, traveled to Mexico to investigate the phenomenon. Biologists thought that sharks needed to swim constantly in order to survive, but these sharks remained motionless inside the caves for extended periods. To obtain oxygen, they pumped water over their gills while they remained stationary. Clark noticed that freshwater was leaking into the caves, lowering the salt concentration. She suggested the change in salinity caused a trancelike state in the sharks. Her team also noticed that *remoras* could easily remove all the parasites from the sharks' skin while in the less salty water. The question of whether or not sharks or other fish actually sleep, as defined by a distinctive change in brain waves, has never been resolved.

Outreach

As the 1970s drew to a close, pollution threatened many of the world's waters. Clark was particularly concerned with the fate of the Red Sea since one of her favorite places to dive was Ras Muhammad, located at the southern tip of the Sinai Peninsula. She initiated efforts to have the site declared a national park, which would help protect it from the traffic that caused damage to its coral reefs and pollution. Thanks to her efforts, the vision became a reality in 1983, and the park now is often referred to as an underwater Garden of Eden.

In 1981, on the coast of Baja California, Clark took her first ride on a whale shark. These gentle creatures grow up to 40 feet (12 m) long and eat mostly plankton. Later she would discourage others from doing the same, to leave the sea creatures in peace.

From 1987 to 1990, Clark was the chief scientist for the Beebe Project, funded by National Geographic. She was in charge of 71 dives in deep-ocean submersibles, underwater vessels that can travel distances of up to 20,000 feet (6 km). Her longest dive was 17.5

hours and her deepest was to 12,000 feet (3,658 m). She also served as a consultant for several television specials about marine life, including *The Sharks* in 1982, a program that was sponsored by National Geographic and received the highest Nielsen rating for a television documentary. She wrote a children's book, *The Desert Beneath the Sea*, in 1991 with author Ann McGovern. That same year, she visited Ningaloo Reef Marine Park in Australia to study whale sharks. She saw 200 in a single month and observed their eating habits. Though she retired from the University of Maryland as a professor emerita in 1992, she still has an office there and continues to travel to exotic locations around the world. During the spring of 2004, Clark went on a research expedition in the South Pacific. She married a longtime friend, Henry Yoshinobu Kon, in 1997.

In a career that has spanned seven decades, Clark has contributed significantly to knowledge in the fields of fish and shark behavior, taxonomy, and ecology. She has discovered 11 new species, authored over 165 scientific and popular articles about marine science, and consulted for or participated in over 200 radio and television programs dealing with conservation marine biology, fishes, diving, and career women. She has received numerous medals and awards for her research. The NGS, the Society of Women Geographers, the Maryland Women's Hall of Fame, the American Society of Oceanographers, and other organizations have acknowledged her. The University of Massachusetts awarded her an honorary doctorate degree in 1992, and the University of Guelph and Long Island University awarded her honorary doctorates in 1995. Four new fish species bear names in her honor: *Callogobius clarki, Sticharium clarkae, Enneapterygius clarkae,* and *Atrobucca geniae.* She remains committed to teaching others to protect and appreciate marine life.

CHRONOLOGY

1922	Eugenie Clark is born on May 4 in New York, New York
1942	Receives a bachelor's degree in zoology from Hunter College
1942–46	Works as a chemist at Celanese Corporation of America

1946	Earns a master's degree in zoology from NYU. Works with Carl Hubbs at Scripps Institution of Oceanography in California and learns to dive
1949	Studies fish in the South Seas for the U.S. Navy
1950	Earns a doctorate in zoology from NYU and receives a Fulbright scholarship to study fish in the Red Sea
1953	Publishes autobiography, *Lady with a Spear*
1955	Founds and becomes executive director of Cape Haze Marine Laboratory (now Mote Marine Laboratory)
1958	Performs research on shark learning
1967	Leaves Cape Haze Marine Laboratory
1968	Joins the department of zoology at the University of Maryland
1969	Publishes second autobiography, *The Lady and the Sharks*
1972	Studies the garden eel and Moses sole in the Red Sea and starts writing for *National Geographic* magazine
1973	Is promoted to full professor of zoology at the University of Maryland
1975	Studies phenomenon of sleeping sharks in Mexico
1979	Begins conservation efforts in the Red Sea
1987	Becomes chief scientist of the Beebe Project and starts making submersible dives
1992	Becomes professor emerita at the University of Maryland but continues teaching, research, and writing
1999	Retires from teaching but continues to dive and study fish and sharks

FURTHER READING

Butts, Ellen R., and Joyce Schwartz. *Eugenie Clark: Adventures of a Shark Scientist.* North Haven, Conn.: Linnet Books, 2000. Life story of the ichthyologist, writer, diver, and teacher.

Dr. Eugenie Clark Web site. Available online. URL: http://www.sharklady.com. Accessed on January 19, 2005. Contains links to her résumé, biographical resources, frequently asked questions, and an interview with National Public Radio.

Mote Marine Laboratory. Available online. URL: http://www.mote.org. Last updated on January 18, 2005. Contains links to sites about the lab, its history, current research, and educational programs.

Polking, Kirk. *Oceanographers and Explorers of the Sea.* Springfield, N.J.: Enslow, 1999. Profiles 10 marine scientists whose specialties range from biology to physical geology. Appropriate for middle and high school students.

Reis, Ronald A. *Eugenie Clark: Marine Biologist.* New York: Facts On File, 2005. Provides career information on marine biologists and divers through this exciting story.

Stone, Tanya Lee. *Scientists: Their Lives and Works.* Vol. 7. Detroit: U*X*L, 2002. Alphabetically arranged introductions to the contributions of scientists from a variety of fields. Intended for middle school students.

9

Sylvia Earle

(1935–)

Sylvia Earle uses her expert knowledge of ocean ecology to advocate oceanic conservation. *(Courtesy of OAR/National Undersea Research Program)*

Pioneer of Scuba Use for Marine Research

Not many people know what they want to do with their lives before they must choose a college major, even fewer before entering elementary school. Pioneering American oceanographer Sylvia Earle was called to the sea at age three when she was knocked over by a wave while wading on the shore. Instead of crying, she laughed and got back on her feet, ready to face more. She has harbored this same fearless attitude throughout her career, while setting deep diving records and advocating public education about the oceans. She was one of the first marine scientists to use scuba as an integral part of her research program and has identified many new marine species. Her area of expertise is *phycology*, or the study of algae, but she is just as comfortable swimming with 40-ton whales. Having logged 7,000 hours underwater, Earle has been aptly named, "Her Deepness."

From a Farm to the Coast

Sylvia Alice Reade Earle was born on August 30, 1935, in Gibbstown, New Jersey. Her father, Lewis Reade Earle, an electrical contractor, and her mother, Alice Freas Richie Earle, raised her to appreciate the natural world. As the middle child of three siblings, Sylvia enjoyed exploring the pond, creek, and orchard around her family's home, a farm outside Paulsboro, New Jersey. She knew very early on that she wanted to become a biologist and spent afternoons making observations and taking notes concerning the wildlife around the farm.

When she was 12 years old, the family moved to Dunedin, Florida, into a house with the Gulf of Mexico in the backyard. As a birthday present that year, Sylvia received a gift of swim goggles. She enjoyed reading books by her favorite author, naturalist William Beebe, and yearned to see the creatures he described. Her first diving experience was with a friend and her friend's father in the Weekiwatchee River. The copper helmet that she wore was attached to an air compressor on shore. After 20 minutes the air pump stopped working properly, and she had to be rescued, but she had been so enthralled watching a school of fish that she did not let this experience deter her from going under again.

Algal Expert

Sylvia enrolled in a summer marine biology course taught by Dr. Harold Humm at Florida State University (FSU) when she was 17 years old. She learned to use scuba gear and loved gliding underwater, following the fish. After earning a bachelor's degree from

FSU in 1955, she applied and was accepted to several prestigious graduate programs. She selected Duke University in Durham, North Carolina, where she was awarded a full scholarship and where Dr. Humm was working. As a master's candidate, she majored in botany but focused on algae and became the first person to systematically study the algae in the Gulf of Mexico, amassing a collection with over 20,000 specimens. She received a master's degree in botany in 1956, at only 20 years of age.

That same year she married zoologist John (Jack) Taylor. They moved to Dunedin, next door to Earle's parents and set up a makeshift lab complete with specimen cabinets and microscopes in their garage. Their daughter Elizabeth was born in 1960 and their son John (called Richie) in 1962.

In 1964 Earle toured the Indian Ocean on the *Anton Bruun*, for an expedition sponsored by the National Science Foundation (NSF). The marine botanist who was scheduled to go had can-celled, and Humm recommended Earle as a replacement on the six-week trip. Though some thought it was bad luck to have a woman on the ship, the 70 members of the all-male crew were impressed with her hard work. She spent as much time as possible exploring underwater and discovered a new species of bright pink algae that reminded her of something Dr. Suess would invent. She named it *Hummbrella hydra* in honor of her mentor. Over the next two years, she went on four more expeditions on the *Anton Bruun* and became acquainted with the famous ichthyologist Eugenie Clark.

Researching the role of algae in marine food chains for 10 years familiarized Earle with the far-reaching effects of pollution on aquatic plant life. In 1966 she completed her dissertation, "Phaeophyta of the Eastern Gulf of Mexico." With a Ph.D. in botany from Duke, she assumed a temporary position as resident director of the Cape Haze Marine Laboratories, founded by Clark, in Sarasota. The following year she accepted simultaneous positions as a research scholar at the Radcliffe Institute and a research fellow at the Farlow Herbarium at Harvard University, which houses algae, fungi, and bryophyte specimens. (Harvard promoted her to researcher in 1975.) She was particularly inter-ested in ocean ecology, the relationship between plants and

Algae

The term *algae* refers to a large and diverse group of *eukaryotic photosynthetic* organisms that can harvest energy from sunlight and convert it to chemical energy. Algae live in fresh or salt water, may be single-celled or multicellular, flaunt a variety of colors and structures, and range in size from microscopic to 200 feet (60 m) in length. Ecologically, they are a very important part of aquatic food chains because they are primary producers of organic substances, and thus, serve as food for fish and other marine animals. Through *photosynthesis,* they also produce oxygen necessary for other organisms.

Some algae bear a resemblance to plants, while others appear more similar to protozoa. There are six divisions of algae. Green algae, *chlorophyta,* are the most well-known and the most diverse with over 7,000 species, mostly freshwater. Scientists believe chlorophyta, which contain the pigment *chlorophyll,* are the evolutionary precursor to land plants. Scum that grows over ponds and lakes belongs to this division. Red algae, *rhodophyta,* have a pigment named phycoerythrin that reflects red light and absorbs blue. Because wavelengths of blue light penetrate deeper than those of red light, red algae can live at great depths. One type of red algae, coralline algae, secretes a carbonate shell around itself, and thus contributes significantly to reef construction. The brown algae,

animals with each other and with their environment, and studied these relationships by making numerous dives. On one such dive in 1968, Earle dove to 100 feet (30 m) below the surface in the submersible *Deep Diver;* she was four months pregnant with her daughter Gale from her second marriage at the time. (She had divorced Taylor and married an ichthyologist from Harvard named Giles Mead.)

phaeophyta, are almost all marine and flourish in cold ocean waters. Brown kelps are the longest known algae. The division *chrysophyta* includes golden algae and diatoms, whose shells look like beautifully cut, tiny pieces of glass with elaborate patterns. *Pyrrophyta,* also called *dinoflagellates,* are an important constituent of plankton. The phenomenon of red tide is caused by outbreaks of the dinoflagellate *Gymnidinium breve* (among others). The last division, euglenophyta, are freshwater, unicellular, motile organisms.

Not only are algae ecologically important, but they are also economically significant. Brown algae and red algae serve as a major food source in Asia. In Japan, the red alga *Porphyra,* also called nori, is used to make sushi and is added to soup. Other red algae are eaten as vegetables or as sweet jellies. The brown seaweed known as kelp contains many vitamins and other nutritional supplements such as iodine. The manufacture of toothpastes, cosmetics, and foods such as ice cream depends on thickening agents extracted from kelps. Microbiologists use agar, which is extracted from the cell walls of some red algae, to make solid growth media, and pharmaceutical corporations use it to encapsulate drugs.

Though a vital part of marine food chains, algae can also be harmful. Overgrowth into algal blooms may result from the presence of excess nutrients in sewage plant discharges or suburban runoff. Under these nutrient rich conditions, the algae thrive and then die. As the algae decompose, the available oxygen is depleted from the water, harming other life-forms.

Underwater Habitat

One day Earle saw an announcement on the bulletin board at Harvard requesting proposals for underwater research for Tektite II. Tektite I was a government experiment that put four scientists 50 feet (15 m) underwater in an enclosed habitat near the Virgin Islands for 60 days in 1969. The goals of the Tektite II project were

Earle led an all-female Tektite II team, shown here training in 1970. *(Courtesy of OAR/National Undersea Research Program and National Park Service)*

to determine the limitations and practicality of saturation diving and to study undersea habitats, but the National Aeronautics and Space Administration (NASA) was also interested in how people handled living together in tight quarters in an unusual environment. Earle's qualifications and proposal for studying the influence of herbivorous fish on marine plants were impressive. At 1,000 hours, she had more hours of diving experience than all the other applicants, but the navy was not prepared for the fact that she was a woman. They decided to hire Earle to lead an all-female team of oceanographers to live in an underwater chamber for two weeks in 1970.

The underwater habitat had carpet, television, bunk beds, showers, and a stove for cooking frozen meals. The upstairs work area had microscopes and a communications panel. A ladder led down to a chamber through which the divers entered the water. Air pressure prevented water from flowing up into the living quarters. NASA psychologists monitored the five scientists constantly and recorded their activities every six minutes. Earle's favorite time to explore was in the predawn darkness, and she especially enjoyed observing the behavior of individual fish. As part of their experiments, Earle and another team member tested *rebreathers* instead of scuba tanks. Rebreathers were more expensive and complicated to prepare, but they allowed the divers to stay underwater for four hours rather than one and were quieter, so they could hear the fish grunt and chew on coral.

At the end of two weeks, the five scientists had to spend 19 hours in a decompression chamber to allow their bodies to readjust to normal atmospheric pressure. Earle had documented 154 species of plants, including 26 species never before seen in the Virgin Islands. In addition to confirming that herbivorous fish greatly affected marine plant populations, she learned the sleeping habits of different types of fish and realized that individual fish had food preferences just like people. The mission stimulated a lot of publicity to which Earle had difficulty adjusting at first, but she decided to use it to her advantage in order to reach the masses with a message about the dangers of ocean pollution. She used her newfound fame to begin writing for *National Geographic* magazine and to produce films that aroused public interest in marine biology. She hoped that greater understanding about the oceans would lead to more caring and positive action toward her goal of protecting them.

Swimming with Humpbacks

In 1976 Earle became a research biologist and curator at the California Academy of Sciences and a fellow in botany at the Natural History Museum of the University of California at Berkeley (UCB). Her marriage to Mead had ended, and she had moved to California. She began a project studying humpback whales during the winter of 1977 in collaboration with Roger and Katy Payne, who were experts on these whales that migrate from Hawaii where they mate and give birth to Alaska where they feed each summer. At the time, most of what was known about whales had been learned from examining carcasses, but Earle knew she could learn much more by studying them in their natural environment. In the 1960s, Roger Payne had set up a microphone in the sea in hopes of recording sounds the whales made and captured scores of songs composed of creaks, grunts, and moans. Biologists have since learned that only males produce the distinct melodies that last up to 20 minutes and can be heard at a distance of 20 miles (32 km). When in the water, the vibrations from the whales' songs made Earle's body vibrate. By following the whales, Earle learned to recognize individual whales by distinctive markings on their faces, flippers, tails, and undersides. Earle collaborated with Payne and filmmaker Al Giddings to produce a documentary film about the humpbacks, *Gentle Giants of the Pacific*, that described the role whales play in the oceanic ecosystem.

Record-Breaking Dives

The next adventure involved a *Jim suit*, which resembled space attire and allowed a person to walk on the ocean floor. Jim suits were typically used for people making repairs to underwater machines or oil rigs; a scientist had never used one for research purposes. Giddings thought it would be remarkable to film Earle outfitted in one strolling along the ocean bottom at 1,000 feet (305 m) for an upcoming television special. The garments were made of magnesium, a malleable metal that could withstand the intense water pressure at great depths, and had steel pincers as hands. A cable connected the suit's wearer with a submersible that followed behind.

Earle welcomed the challenge, and on October 19, 1979, she set a record for free-diving at 1,250 feet (381 m). In the Jim suit, she walked stiffly along the ocean floor and jotted down observations she made while watching the giant seven-foot (2.1-m) rays and long-legged crabs with whom she shared her pedway. She also admired pink sea fans, jellyfish, a cat shark, lantern fish, hatchetfish, and bamboo coral that rippled with gleaming blue rings when nudged. Her two and one-half hour time limit passed quickly, but before returning to the submersible platform for ascension, she planted two flags to mark the historic moment in the ocean floor, a U.S. flag and a National Geographic flag. Since then, more advanced submersibles have replaced the Jim suits for many purposes.

JIM SUIT

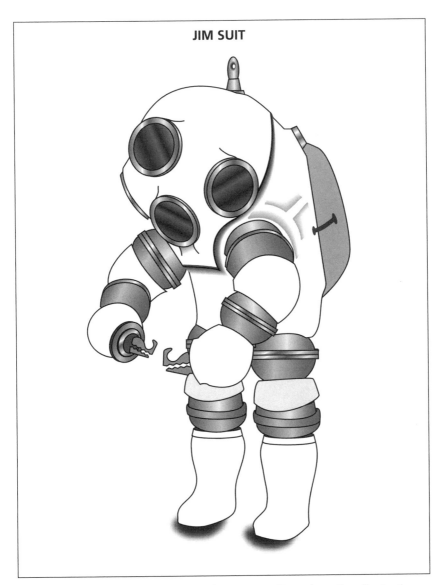

The inside of the Jim suit is pressurized to protect divers from the effects of water pressure at depths nearing 2,000 feet (610 m).

Though Earle was thrilled to have set a new free-diving record, she yearned to go deeper since the average depth of the ocean is 13,000 feet (3,962 m). In a joint venture in 1982, Earle and British-born engineer Graham Hawkes (to whom she was married from 1986–89) founded a company called Deep Ocean Technology (later called Deep Ocean Engineering), to build state-of-the-art, deep-diving, one-man submersibles. One major obstacle they had to overcome was choosing a material that could withstand the pressure at great depths but was transparent to allow observation. Customers were hard to find, so Hawkes built a large *remotely operated vehicle* (ROV) that could be used to inspect undersea equipment. After selling one to Shell Oil Company, they started receiving more orders. In 1984 they made *Deep Rover*, a spherical submersible with mechanical arms that held one diver and operated at record-breaking depths of 3,000 feet (914 m). Earle went down in *Deep Rover* at night, an experience she compared to falling into a fireworks display because of the luminescent creatures floating around her. Her mesmerizing experience observing jellies, shrimp, interesting fish, and an octopus was marred by the sight of a soda can on the ocean floor. Today Deep Ocean Engineering continues to design and manufacture ROVs that are sold internationally.

A Mission to Preserve

President George H. W. Bush appointed Earle chief scientist at the National Oceanic and Atmospheric Administration (NOAA) in 1990. NOAA is a U.S. governmental organization whose mission is to describe and predict changes in the Earth's environment and to conserve and manage the nation's coastal and marine resources. Earle was initially worried about not being able to voice her opinions in public as an upper level government representative, but she accepted the opportunity in hopes of eliciting change. She had become increasingly aggravated at the government's apathy about undersea exploration and its unwillingness to invest money for undersea research.

In 1991, as chief scientist of an underwater research team, Earle investigated the aftermath of 500 million gallons (over two billion liters) of oil that Iraq deliberately dumped into the Persian Gulf during the Gulf War. Her task was to figure out how long it would take the ocean and its inhabitants to recover from the devastating effects. The landscape was completely blackened for miles, and the waters were oily and brown. Seeing the marine organisms covered in black slime reaffirmed her commitment to spreading the message of ocean conservation. She also investigated the effects on the ecosystems in Prince William Sound, Alaska, of the oil spills from the ship *Exxon Valdez*. She resigned from NOAA after 18 months.

In 1992 Earle founded Deep Ocean Engineering Research (DOER) with her daughter, Elizabeth Taylor. Located in Alameda, California, DOER's mission is to promote ocean exploration and conservation.

Earle accompanied Japanese scientists on an expedition in 1991, when she descended in a three-man submersible named *Shinkai 6500* to 13,000 feet (almost 4 km), deeper than she had ever been before. The Japanese government asked Earle to lend her expertise for building a remote, then manned, submersible that could dive to 36,000 feet (11 km) in 1993.

In 1995 Earle used her reputation as an expert of the deep ocean to champion conservation by publishing a book, *Sea Change: A Message of the Oceans*, that celebrated the variety and abundance of life below the sea's surface. Along with her fascination, she also soberly shared her worries about the future of the oceans in the hands of uninformed humans.

The National Geographic Society (NGS) named Earle explorer-in-residence in 1998. From 1998 to 2002 she served as project director for the Sustainable Seas Expeditions, supported by the NGS, the NOAA, and the Goldman Foundation, to explore and document the marine life and conditions of the 12 U.S. marine sanctuaries. A comprehensive survey of these underwater national parks will allow marine scientists to detect changes to the ecosystems and make recommendations for the preservation of their health. During this time she also published *Wild Ocean* (1999) and *Atlas of the Ocean* (2001).

Earle has led more than 60 expeditions and logged more than 7,000 hours underwater. She has earned numerous honors and awards and received a dozen honorary degrees from institutions, including Florida International University, the Monterey Institute, Duke, the University of Connecticut, and the University of Rhode Island. She is a member of the American Association of the Academy of Sciences, the California Academy of Sciences, the

Marine Technology Society, and the World Academy of Arts and Sciences. She serves on boards and committees for Woods Hole Oceanographic Institute, Mote Marine Laboratory, the World Wildlife Fund, and many more. In 2000 she was inducted into the National Women's Hall of Fame. The sea urchin *Diadema sylvie* and the red alga *Pilina earli* were named in her honor.

Time magazine aptly named Earle the first "hero for the planet" in 1998. Her authorship of over 125 publications about marine science earned her the right to speak on behalf of the oceans and to educate the public about the oceans and marine life. As an ambassador for the sea, she has strongly and repeatedly expressed the opinion that if people knew about marine life, they would care more about protecting it. Living up to this responsibility, she has made more than 100 television appearances in interviews and in special programs. It is the world's responsibility to respond to her challenge.

CHRONOLOGY

1935	Sylvia Earle is born on August 30 in Gibbstown, New Jersey
1955	Receives a bachelor of science degree in marine botany from Florida State University
1956	Receives a master's degree in botany from Duke University
1964	Joins NSF expedition to the Indian Ocean on *Anton Bruun*
1966	Receives a doctorate degree in botany from Duke University
1967–69	Is Radcliffe Institute scholar
1967–81	Works as research fellow, then research associate, at Harvard University
1968	Travels 100 feet (30 m) below the ocean surface in the Bahamas in the submersible *Deep Diver*
1969–81	Is a research associate at the UCB
1970	Leads the Tektite II mission, for which an all-female team lived in an enclosed undersea habitat for two weeks

1976	Becomes research biologist and curator at the California Academy of Sciences and a fellow in botany at the Natural History Museum of the UCB
1977	Begins studying humpback whales
1979	Walks in pressurized suit on ocean floor at a record depth of 1,250 feet (381 m) off Oahu, Hawaii
1979-86	Serves as curator of phycology at the California Academy of Sciences
1982	Founds Deep Ocean Technology (later Deep Ocean Engineering) with Graham Hawkes
1984	Earle and others dive to a record-breaking 3,280 feet (1 km) in the deep-sea submersible *Deep Rover*
1990-92	Serves as chief scientist of the NOAA
1992	Founds Deep Ocean Exploration and Research to design robotic sub sea systems
1995	Authors *Sea Change: A Message of the Oceans*
1998	Named explorer-in-residence for the NGS
1998-2002	Leads the Sustainable Seas Expeditions, a program to study the National Marine Sanctuary System sponsored by the NGS, NOAA, and the Goldman Foundation
1999	Publishes *Wild Ocean*
2001	Publishes *The Atlas of the Ocean*

FURTHER READING

Baker, Beth. *Sylvia Earle: Guardian of the Sea*. Minneapolis, Minn.: Lerner Publications, 2001. Standard biography written for young adults.

Saari, Peggy, and Stephen Allison, eds. *The Lives and Works of 150 Scientists*. Vol. 1. Detroit: U*X*L, 1996. Alphabetically arranged introductions to the contributions of scientists from a variety of fields. Intended for middle school students.

Stanley, Phyllis M. *American Environmental Heroes*. Springfield, N.J.: Enslow, 1996. Profiles 10 Americans who have helped identify and shape environmental issues and policies. Written for middle school students.

"Sylvia Earle, Ph.D., Undersea Explorer." Part of the Hall of Science and Exploration of the Gallery of Achievement, Academy of Achievement. Available online. URL: http://www. achievement.org/autodoc/page/ear0bio-1. Last revised on November 5, 2001. A biography with link to an interview with Dr. Earle.

10

Robert D. Ballard

(1942–)

Robert Ballard made major discoveries in marine geology and biology and helped advance technology for deep-sea exploration. *(Hank Morgan/Photo Researchers, Inc.)*

Discovery of Black Smokers and Advancement of Deep-Sea Exploration Techniques

Though he achieved popular fame by his discovery of the RMS *Titanic* and other sunken vessels, Robert Ballard first received praise from his scientific colleagues as a marine geologist. Even before he earned a doctorate degree, his widespread reputation as an authority on deep-sea exploration technology earned him the privilege of becoming the first American and the second scientist to dive into the Mid-Atlantic Ridge, dubbed the center of creation, to explore volcanic and tectonic processes. A few years later, Dr. Ballard found *hydrothermal vents*, cracks in the seafloor that spouted mineral-rich, hot water. The unique conditions created environments compatible with the establishment of tiny ecosystems that have provided biologists with startling information about the origin of life. During a 27-year career at the Woods Hole Oceanographic Institute (WHOI), he founded the Deep Submergence Laboratory and became director of the Center for Marine Exploration, where he developed both manned and unmanned submergence technology. His interests gradually shifted toward maritime history and marine archeology, a field that he has helped establish as a new science. As founder of the JASON project, a Web-based distant educational program for high school students, and as current president of the Institute for Exploration, Ballard continues to make contributions to ocean exploration.

California Boyhood

Robert Duane Ballard was born on June 30, 1942, to Chester and Harriet Nell May Ballard in Wichita, Kansas. His father's career as a flight test engineer brought the family to California when Robert and his older brother Richard were very young. Later the Ballards had a daughter named Nancy. Growing up near the San Diego suburb of Pacific Beach, Bob often explored tidal pools on the shores of Mission Bay, sometimes using his mother's glass bowls to see more clearly under the water. After reading *Twenty Thousand Leagues Under the Sea* by Jules Verne, Bob was entranced by the deep ocean. He was athletic in high school and made decent grades. As a senior, he won a National Science Foundation competition for a position in a summer oceanography research program at the Scripps Institution of Oceanography (SIO), part of the University of California at San Diego. Despite almost sinking during a hurricane while on an expedition at sea, ocean research enthralled him.

After graduating from Downey High School in 1960, Bob entered the University of California at Santa Barbara, where he joined a fraternity, played sports, and entered the U.S. Army ROTC (Reserve Officers' Training Corps) program. Enrolled in a demanding physical sciences curriculum, Bob's grades suffered during his third year, and though his strong desire for a career in oceanography compelled him to buckle down, SIO rejected his application for their doctoral program. Feeling dejected, Bob enrolled in business and accounting courses at the University of California at Los Angeles during the summer of 1964, but that fall he sent out applications to numerous oceanography graduate programs. The University of Hawaii accepted him, and after completing his undergraduate degree in geology and chemistry in January 1965, he moved to Honolulu.

Thwarted Career Plans

While in graduate school, Ballard worked as a *cetacean* trainer for Sea Life Park, a trained animal center and theater. Fascinated by the images of undersea geological features, he decided to specialize in marine geology. Thinking the navy was a more appropriate branch of military service considering his interests, he transferred his army commission. In 1966 the Ocean Systems Group of North American Aviation gave Ballard a full-time position developing missions for their first manned submersible and offered to pay for his doctoral studies at the University of Southern California (USC). He moved to Long Beach, married Marjorie Hargas, whom he had met in Hawaii, enrolled at USC, and started working toward what he believed would develop into a distinguished industrial marine science career.

Unaware that Ballard was still in graduate school or that he was married, the navy disrupted his future plans by calling him to active duty. After getting special permission to complete his semester at USC, in March of 1967, Ballard and his new wife set out for Boston, Massachusetts, where he served in the Office of Naval Research (ONR). His duties included acting as a liaison to WHOI, a research facility in Cape Cod devoted to ocean science that received funding from the navy. Disappointed that he had to interrupt his graduate studies and worried that he might not be able to return to them after his commission expired, Ballard found some consolation in being introduced to *Alvin*, WHOI's small submersible used for biological and physical research of the ocean's bottom. Dr. Kenneth O. Emery, a renowned marine geologist and expert on the history and structure of the sedimentary rocks of the North American *continental margins*, encouraged Ballard not to give up on graduate school and promised to keep him involved in the field by inviting him on future research cruises.

Emery was true to his word, and in September of 1967, Ballard participated in a three-week geological survey of the rise off the northern Atlantic seaboard. Unlike land geologists, marine geologists cannot slice open rock formations to look at exposed layers or collect samples with a simple hammer and chisel. Instead they must rely on sophisticated instruments such as *seismic profilers* that use echo sounding to locate submerged landforms. A sound wave generator blasts huge pulses of energy, some of which penetrate into the sediments before being reflected back to the surface by hard rock. Marine geologists use this information collected by a graphic recorder, as well as other data relating to magnetic and gravitational fields, to construct a geological map of the structure of the ocean floor. During his first cruise for WHOI, Ballard learned how to use the dozens of instruments, carefully monitoring the machines and logging information.

The amount of information gathered during a three-week cruise could take a year to evaluate. WHOI marine geologist Dr. Al Uchupi offered Ballard the opportunity to analyze data from reams of depth-sounding data collected from the Gulf of Mexico. Knowing this was a valuable learning opportunity for an aspiring scientist, Ballard undertook the challenge and spent months pouring over the data, drawing conclusions, and writing it all up in the form of a scientific paper. The experience turned out to be even more educational than he anticipated; Emery and Bill Rainnie, the full-time project manager for WHOI's Deep Submergence Group, both harshly criticized his commingling of results and conclusions. A scientific writer must present results clearly and objectively, separate from any conclusions or interpretations. His mentors explained that though his conclusions might or might not be correct, facts were facts and might be valuable to future analyses. Though it was not a milestone in geology, Ballard's informative revised paper, "Morphology and Quaternary History of the Continental Shelf of the Gulf Coast of the United States" appeared in the *Bulletin of Marine Science* in 1970.

In 1969 Ballard made the decision to leave the navy, but in order to enter a career of academic research, he still needed a doctorate degree. Rainnie gave Ballard a job soliciting customers for *Alvin*, and Emery helped Ballard make the necessary contacts to enroll as a graduate student in marine geology at the University of Rhode Island. This arrangement allowed Ballard to complete the remainder of his coursework in Rhode Island but perform his thesis research at WHOI.

Geological Evidence for Plate Tectonics

The early 1970s were an exciting time for marine geology. The theory of continental displacement, first proposed by Alfred Wegener in 1912, had evolved into the theory of plate tectonics, which states that the continents and the ocean crust are embedded in and ride on seven major granite rock plates (there are also as many as 12 smaller ones) that float over a layer of dense, semi-molten magma. Once part of a single enormous supercontinent, the seven modern continental landmasses have drifted apart over millions of years, forming today's oceans. The discovery of seafloor spreading by Harry Hammond Hess in the early 1960s provided a mechanism for continental movement. At mid-oceanic ridges, such as the Mid-Atlantic Ridge that is part of a monstrous mountain system approximately 40,000 miles (64,000 km) long, molten magma rises up from the Earth's mantle, creating new seafloor. At the oceanic trenches, old oceanic crust recycles into the deep Earth near the continental borders in a process called *subduction.*

Ballard wanted to do research on plate tectonics for his doctoral thesis research project. Geologists believe that the Atlantic Ocean formed early in the Mesozoic Era, which occurred 225 to 65 million years ago, when the North American and African tectonic plates separated. Ballard looked for evidence of plate separation by studying the geology of a formation of Appalachian Mountains that extended offshore into the continental shelf in the Gulf of Maine, north of Cape Cod. After obtaining surface surveys to locate places

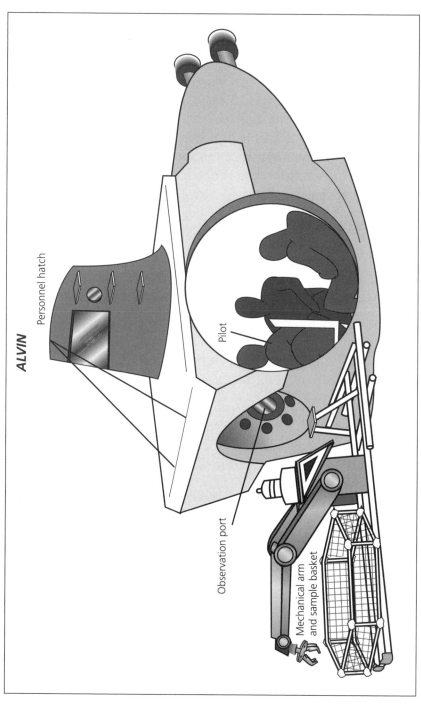

ALVIN

Personnel hatch

Pilot

Observation port

Mechanical arm
and sample basket

Having undergone many upgrades over the years, today *Alvin* can carry three passengers to depths of more than 14,000 feet (4,267 m), remain submerged for 10 hours under normal conditions, and collect biological and geological samples that are stored in a basket in front of the sub.

where bedrock protruded from the sediment, he used *Alvin* to collect rock samples for analysis. *Alvin* was 22 feet (6.7 m) long, contained a six-foot 10-inch (2.08-m) diameter spherical vessel that held three people during dives and mechanical arms for retrieving geological samples from the ocean floor. From 1971 to 1972, Ballard went on dozens of dives with *Alvin* to survey the submerged mountain group and the surrounding rock. The results led to his dissertation, "The Behavior of the Gulf of Maine and Adjacent Region During Continental Collision and Subsequent Separation," showing that the geological structure formed during a 100-million-year period spanning the late Triassic and early Jurassic Periods, when the Atlantic Ocean was born. He successfully defended his doctoral dissertation in June of 1974.

The Center of Creation

Though Ballard had toddler sons, Todd, born in 1968, and Douglas, born in 1970, he was rarely at home. Expeditions at sea, research at the WHOI library, and soliciting customers for *Alvin* consumed his time. His reputation as an authority on the use of deep-towed vehicles and manned submersibles was growing. French marine geophysicist Dr. Xavier Le Pichon sought WHOI's expertise for a project whose goal was to explore the central rift valley in the Mid-Atlantic Ridge. Ballard learned all he could about volcanism and basaltic rock before the French-American Mid-Ocean Undersea Study (FAMOUS) commenced. The 9,000-foot (2,700-m) valley exhibited a typical volcanic rift structure and marked the separation points of the North American and African tectonic plates. During the summer of 1972, scientists used sonar and seismic surveys to construct a bathymetric map of the target site.

On August 4, 1973, Pichon dove down in the French navy's bathysphere *Archimède*. The following day, despite a worsening respiratory infection, Ballard became the second scientist and the first American to dive on the Mid-Atlantic Ridge. In an effort to document how the seafloor split and spread apart, he visually explored the glistening black lava flows and collected samples of the basaltic rock believed to have been extruded from beneath the seafloor.

Near the end of Ballard's dive, an electrical fire filled the chamber with smoke. When he put on his emergency oxygen mask, his lungs screamed in pain, and he ripped it back off. The fellow divers thought he was panicking and forced the mask back on, until they realized that the valve controlling the flow of oxygen to his mask had never been opened.

Operational since 1964, the first manned deep-sea submersible, *Alvin,* proved to be a reliable and valuable research tool for WHOI. *(Courtesy of OAR/National Undersea Research Program and WHOI)*

The following summer, Ballard returned to the Mid-Atlantic Ridge and used *Alvin*, whose steel sphere was replaced with stronger but lighter titanium, to document additional evidence of tectonic activity. The dive team observed volcanic domes, numerous linear fissures, and recent lava extrusions, all confirming that tectonic activity was driving apart the huge North American and African crustal plates at that site. From inside *Alvin*, Ballard stared directly into a 20-foot (6-m) wide crack, a seemingly bottomless opening leading into deep Earth. FAMOUS resulted in the collection of more than 3,000 pounds (1,360 kg) of geologic samples, 100,000 photographs, and boxes of graphic recordings that would take a decade to analyze. Scientists later estimated that the crustal plates were separating at a rate of about one inch (2.5 cm) per year; given 260 million years, this seemingly slow rate would have resulted in a separation between plates approximately equal to the width of the North Atlantic Ocean.

Ballard published the first of a series of articles for *National Geographic* magazine, "Dive into the Great Rift," in 1975. He described diving in *Alvin* into the Mid-Atlantic Ridge for a general audience.

In Search of Hot Water

From 1976 to 1977, Ballard served as chief scientist on an expedition in the *Knorr* to the Cayman Trough, where two tectonic plates meet. Using sonar bathymetric maps and ANGUS, a camera on a sled that Ballard nicknamed a "dope-on-a-rope," the scientific team collected distinctive samples of igneous rock from the upper mantle. Off the South American Pacific coast, Ballard joined an expedition looking for hydrothermal vents in the Galápagos Rift in 1977. The crew noticed a temperature anomaly that at first they assumed was a glitch in the instrumentation. Geologists believed that mountains on land formed from buckling under pressure but that underwater, heat played a more prominent role in sculpting mountains. Water at depths where ANGUS was gliding, approximately 9,000 feet (2,700 m), typically registered 36.5°F (2.5°C), but the Galápagos Rift was spreading faster than the Mid-Atlantic Ridge, and molten magma was rising to fill the gap. Evidence of hot water was interesting to the marine geologists and geophysicists on board the *Knorr*, who were trying to understand the flow of heat energy from inside the Earth through the crustal plates. The chance was greater of finding hydrothermal circulation in the faster-spreading Pacific Ocean than the Atlantic.

After three minutes, the temperature returned to normal, but unfortunately, the film from ANGUS would not be collected and developed until the following morning. They expected to see photographic evidence of a fissure or a conical vent in the lava from the pictures taken at the same time as the temperature anomaly occurred. Surprisingly, the photos revealed hundreds of clams surrounded by turbid, milky water. Never expecting to see a thriving colony of living organisms in near-freezing temperatures on a bed of hardened lava, no biologists were aboard the ship. *Alvin* dove into the astonishing clam bed, which they nicknamed "Clambake I," where the temperature registered 61°F (16°C). They retrieved samples of not only the clams, but also the water for chemical analysis. On board, opening the water bottles released a powerful stench of rotten eggs, a telltale odor for hydrogen sulfide, a gas poisonous to most living creatures.

Over the next five weeks, 21 more dives on the rift revealed other colonies of living creatures, including scavenging white crabs, albino lobsters, pink fish, red tubeworms, and flowerlike animals. One location contained only empty clamshells; previously existing warm water vents that supported life in the small, defined surrounding area were no longer present. Though different organisms dominated different sites amid the barren basaltic rocks, all contained hydrogen sulfide that acted as the ultimate source of energy for the little ecosystems. On the ocean's surface and on land, most life depends on sunlight that photosynthetic organisms utilize to make carbohydrates from carbon dioxide, but sunlight cannot penetrate to the ocean floor. *Chemosynthetic prokaryotic* organisms extracted energy from the hydrogen sulfide and used it to synthesize organic compounds that other animals could metabolize for energy. The high concentrations of sulfur around these vents would kill many organisms, but the life-forms that inhabited the hydrothermal vents were uniquely adapted to survive in such an environment.

The discovery of life in isolated oases on the otherwise desolate environment of the ocean floor was both shocking and remarkable. Seawater trickled down into the vents, became superheated, and brought dissolved minerals from within the Earth that allowed life to exist in extreme conditions similar to those that dominated during the early days of the Earth's formation. The implications were astounding—life may have originated under these conditions, and such environments existed elsewhere in the universe. Since this was supposed to be a geophysical and geochemical research cruise, Ballard's crew was not properly equipped to collect biological samples and resorted to stuffing Tupperware and soup tureens with the unique specimens that might provide insight into the origin of life.

Funding for additional explorations was easy to obtain. In 1979 Ballard took crews of marine biologists to the Galápagos Rift, where *Alvin* helped them retrieve numerous interesting organisms, some from entirely new phyla and some that were living fossils. Microbiologists identified over 200 strains of bacteria, and chemists determined that nutrients at the vent sites were present in concentrations 300–500 times greater than outside the vent areas.

Black Smokers

Amidst the excitement accompanying the biological discoveries, an inexperienced scientist on a French expedition in 1978 to the East Pacific Rise, off Mexico's Baja California, had collected a geological sample from an unusual polychrome chimney structure. Unaware of its peculiarity, he packed it away with numerous other samples to be analyzed later. Months passed before researchers identified the sample to be a sulfide of zinc never before found on volcanic seafloor terrain. During Ballard's expedition to the Galápagos Rift, his crew had observed strange tubular deposits, but they crumbled when the crew tried to take samples. In 1979 Ballard was in the East Pacific Rise when divers spotted cylindrical chimney structures, one of which was spouting what looked like black smoke. This could not have been smoke underwater but instead was a rich suspension of minerals. The temperature registered 91°F (32°C), warmer than any water at the Galápagos Rift. After hauling *Alvin* up that night, the scientists saw that the tip of the temperature probe was charred and melted. How hot was it really?

The following day Ballard went down in *Alvin* with a more durable temperature probe, and as he came within about 10 feet (3 m) of a chimney, the temperature measured an unbelievable 662°F (350°C). Observations over the next 12 days revealed both white and *black smokers*, some up to 30 feet (9 m) tall. The chimneys were composed of almost pure crystalline zinc sulfide, and geochemists determined that the seawater maintained its unique chemistry by recycling through fissures and hydrothermal vents. The crew finished exploring the East Pacific Rise using *Alvin* and ANGUS and found a whole new system of hydrothermal vents and animal colonies. Ballard needed some time to contemplate and synthesize all that occurred during his hugely successful decade at Woods Hole.

The RMS *Titanic*

Ballard moved his family to Palo Alto, California, where he spent his sabbatical at Stanford University. While there he wrote several papers on plate tectonics, volcanism, and hydrothermal vent systems, and WHOI granted him tenure. Ballard realized the potential worth of a remotely operated vehicle (ROV) for deep-ocean exploration and began to conceive of the *Argo-Jason* system. *Argo* would be a towed video camera sled whose images would be viewable in real time from shipboard monitors. *Jason* would be an unmanned ROV, with a video camera and its own motors, attached to *Argo* by a fiber-optic tether. Ballard dreamed of using the system to explore the legendary lost *Titanic*.

For 73 years, the wreckage from the *Titanic* lay hidden in a chilly undersea Atlantic graveyard, 12,000 feet (3,658 m) below the surface at an unknown location. As a teenager, Ballard read *A Night to Remember*, a book by Walter Lord that chronicled the events of the fateful night in history, and ever since, he had been intrigued by the possibility of being the one to find it. He believed *Argo-Jason* technology could help him do so.

In 1977 Ballard met Bill Tatum, the head of the *Titanic* Historical Society. The two became friends, and together they narrowed a

The Unsinkable Ship

Hailed as unsinkable, the luxurious Royal Mail Ship *Titanic* left Southampton, England, on its maiden voyage to New York on April 10, 1912. By the fifth day of its journey, the ship's captain, E. J. Smith, had received several warnings of icebergs in the area, but the night seemed calm, and he maintained his fast speed. Shortly before midnight, a lookout noticed an iceberg less than one-quarter of a mile (400 m) away and shouted warnings. Though the ship turned immediately, it was too late, and the lavish ocean liner scraped the side of the giant iceberg. Because the ship weighed 46,000 tons and was traveling swiftly, the impact was hardly felt, and passengers unknowingly played with the ice chucks that fell on deck. At 2:20 A.M. on April 15, 1912, the *Titanic* sunk somewhere southeast of Newfoundland.

The slow realization of the seriousness of the situation and confusion in loading lifeboats compounded the disaster, leading to the tragic deaths of 1,522 passengers and crew members. There were only enough lifeboats for approximately half of the ship's occupants, but even though there was room for 1,178 people, only 711 boarded the boats to be rescued later by the nearby *Carpathia*. At the time, no regulations existed that required wireless communication systems to be manned at all times, and only minutes before the *Titanic's* distress call, the operator of the *Californian*, which was even closer to the *Titanic* than the *Carpathia*, went on break.

search area to 100 square miles (260 km²) based on historical records of radioed positions, the locations of the lifeboats when they were rescued, and logged data about weather and current conditions from other ships that traveled in the same area that night.

Without funding though, finding the *Titanic* remained a fantasy for Ballard. Texas multimillionaire Jack Grimm sponsored three expeditions between 1980 and 1983 but all failed, in Ballard's opinion, because the searches were not scientific enough and were based on an ill-defined search area.

The U.S. Navy had an interest in developing technology like the *Argo-Jason* system to explore the precious wreckage of two lost nuclear-powered submarines. The *Thresher* sunk in 1963 south of Georges Bank, and the *Scorpion,* carrying two nuclear torpedoes, sunk south of the Azores in 1968. The navy needed to know if radiation was leaking from the submarines. With the navy's financial support, Ballard inaugurated the Deep Submergence Laboratory at Woods Hole for the purpose of designing and developing the primary survey vehicle *Argo* and the self-powered ROV *Jason. Argo,* with its three video cameras, would hover above the bottom, while

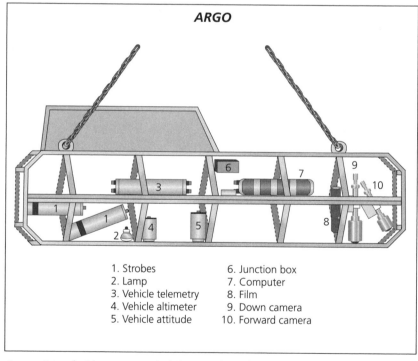

ARGO

1. Strobes
2. Lamp
3. Vehicle telemetry
4. Vehicle altimeter
5. Vehicle attitude
6. Junction box
7. Computer
8. Film
9. Down camera
10. Forward camera

Argo, a towed video camera sled that sends real-time images to a control van, replaced the less sophisticated ANGUS that Ballard referred to as a "dope-on-a-rope."

Jason, with its own lights, cameras, and arms, would be able to explore more places. While Jason was being developed, *Jason Junior*, or *JJ*, would be used to record images.

Ballard tested *Argo* at the *Thresher* site in 1984. The submarine was buried in 8,400 feet (2,560 m) of water, but the sonar and imaging systems worked well, and *Argo* completely mapped the debris field. The use of *telepresence*, watching the *Argo*'s videos in real time, allowed the crew to feel like they were there. While surveying, Ballard became frustrated at not being able to find the end of the debris field. When a ship wrecks in shallow water, the debris covers a circular area, with the center having the main wreckage. He realized that in deep water, the debris fell for a longer period of time, giving the ocean currents an opportunity to move it farther away. After falling to a certain level, the hull would implode from the great water pressure. Heavier debris would fall straight down, relatively unaffected, but lighter debris could be carried as far as one mile before landing on the ocean floor. This should result in a trail of light to heavy, pointing directly to the main wreckage. Using this hypothesis, Ballard was able to locate the hull of the *Thresher*.

The next summer, the navy funded a three-week expedition to explore the *Scorpion*. After four days, Ballard obtained a detailed map of the debris field and the wreckage site, and he was free to spend any remaining time exploring to the west, where the *Titanic* lay. With government endorsement, the French performed a preliminary sonar search of the previously mapped 100-square-mile (260-km^2) area but found nothing. Ballard planned to search for a debris trail, rather than the *Titanic* itself, a strategy that worked for locating both the *Thresher* and the *Scorpion*. *Argo* would "mow the lawn," by scanning east to west, then going north one mile and scanning west to east, and so on. They only had 12 days and no time for mistakes. As the days passed without success, the crew faced annoying equipment glitches and growing pessimism. Then after midnight on September 1, 1985, something angular and steel appeared on the monitor, followed by more metallic debris and sheets of hull plate. The cook happened to be passing by and volunteered to wake up Ballard, who quickly pulled on a jumpsuit over the pajamas that he would wear for the next five days. By the time Ballard arrived, one of the *Titanic*'s distinctive huge boilers appeared on the screen. They had found the famed ship, and everyone was overcome with excitement, but Ballard could not help feeling tremendous sadness at the unnecessary loss of 1,522 human lives. They spent every last minute recording as much video footage and taking as many still photographs as possible, then headed home.

The media was in a frenzy over the discovery, and unavoidable controversies over rights and exclusives, as well as worries about grave-robbing and defacing the underwater gravesite, followed. Ballard managed to keep the exact coordinates of the location secret. The U.S. Navy and the National Geographic Society (NGS) sponsored Ballard's return in July 1986, this time hauling *JJ* beneath *Alvin*. They were able to successfully land *Alvin* on the deck of the *Titanic* and *JJ* freely explored the wreckage, including the famous grand staircase. Ballard's book, *The Discovery of the* Titanic, became an immediate best-seller. The children's version, *Exploring the* Titanic, was also successful.

Shifting Interests

Having experienced several major scientific discoveries firsthand, Ballard wanted to excite children about oceanography and thought bringing telepresence into the classrooms would accomplish his goal of turning students onto science. He established the JASON Project to promote science education by allowing students to participate in research and exploration by transmitting live images from the now fully developed underwater research robot *Jason*. In 1989 JASON I broadcast live to 250,000 students in a dozen museums and classrooms. Ballard first took the students on a tour of the Marsili Seamount, an active underwater volcano northwest of Sicily, where they watched shimmering, mineral-rich water spew from hydrothermal vents. Then *Jason* explored the wreckage of a 1,700-year-old Roman trading vessel in the Mediterranean Sea, shooting images of terra-cotta amphorae that most likely transported wine and olive oil. The students felt as if they were aboard the ship with Ballard's team, and the teachers raved at the project's success.

Every year the JASON Project leads scientists, students, and teachers on a two-week expedition in real time through satellite and Internet contacts. Since 1989 Ballard has explored rainforests, wetlands, humpback whales, volcanoes, coral reefs, hydrothermal vents, and frozen glaciers. *Jason* has visited interesting locations such as Lake Ontario, Hawaii, the Galápagos Islands, the coast of Baja California, and Iceland. Each project integrates several sciences, such as biology, chemistry, geology, physics, oceanography, climatology, history, and archaeology.

Some of Ballard's colleagues teased that he no longer was involved in real science, but Ballard did not care. He knew he was impacting the future careers of the young students involved with JASON. His interests were changing from marine geology to maritime history and marine archeology, and he was making valuable contributions to those fields. In June of 1989, using *Argo*, he located the *Bismarck*, one of Hitler's most powerful warships that was lost during battle in 1941. Ballard's older son, Todd, accompanied him and assisted in the work. Only weeks later, Todd died in a car accident. The news devastated Ballard, and shortly afterward, he and Marjorie divorced.

Ballard married Barbara Hanford Earle, who was in charge of special television projects for NGS, in January 1991. The couple had son William Benjamin Aymar in 1994 and daughter Emily Rose in 1997. Together they founded their own company, Odyssey Corporation. The next year Ballard explored what had been nicknamed Iron Bottom Sound, the location of the Battle of Guadalcanal, in November 1942. The American and Japanese navies both lost 24 warships, and Ballard led the expedition to map the lost fleet. In 1993 he and his wife explored the wreck of the *Lusitania*, a civilian vessel that was torpedoed south of Ireland in 1942. Another famous accomplishment was locating the USS *Yorktown*, a naval aircraft carrier sunk by Japanese torpedoes in 1942 during the Battle of Midway and found under 17,000 feet (over 5 km) of water by Ballard in 1998.

Over the years, Ballard had been promoted up the ranks at WHOI, beginning as a research associate in the geology and geophysics department in 1969, eventually reaching tenured senior

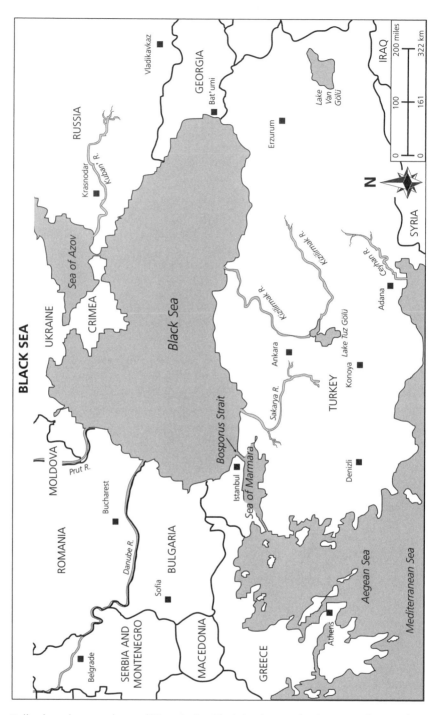

Ballard made several expeditions to the Black Sea in search of ancient shipwrecks and evidence of a great historical flood.

scientist in the department of applied ocean physics and engineering in 1983. In 1997 Ballard retired from WHOI, the home of his numerous extraordinary discoveries in marine geology, geophysics, and deep-sea exploration technology. The governor of Connecticut helped finance a new Institute for Exploration (IFE), headed by Ballard, as an expansion of the Mystic Marine Life Aquarium. IFE specializes in marine archaeology and acts as an avenue for Ballard to share his most recent discoveries in the Challenge of the Deep exhibit. In 2002 Ballard became director of the Institute for Underwater Archaeology at the University of Rhode Island Graduate School in Oceanography.

The Black Sea has been Ballard's destination on several voyages since 1997, when he began exploring the area for ancient shipwrecks. Scientists believed that 10,000 years ago the Black Sea was a freshwater lake. Some believed that as temperatures increased about 7,500 years ago, massive quantities of ice covering the northern hemisphere melted, flooding the Aegean Sea, which poured over the Bosporus Strait into what is now known as the Black Sea. This great flood could be the basis of the catastrophic deluge described in the biblical book of Genesis, which would have occurred about the same time. Other scholars believed the flooding was gradual and occurred earlier than 7,500 years ago. On his expeditions, Ballard found smoothed rocks, evidence of a historical shoreline, and fossil mussels of a species that had been extinct for about 7,000 years.

In order to excavate the region, Ballard designed the remotely piloted submersible *Hercules* that contained lights, cameras, sonar, one powerful arm, and one delicate arm, to simulate the gingerly movements of a human hand. In the summer of 2003, Ballard returned to the Black Sea with *Hercules*, and the mechanical robot proved an efficient tool for ocean archaeological research. The mission unfortunately failed to find any conclusive evidence that the flooding of the Black Sea was a rapid event. Scientists retrieved some wood samples from a suspected human settlement, but carbon dating suggested the pieces floated in to the area after the time of the flood, thus were not useful in showing when the settlement had been built.

Numerous Contributions to a Variety of Fields

Ballard's numerous contributions to the subject of marine science have been recognized by many organizations. To name a few, he received the American Association for the Advancement of Science Newcomb Cleveland Prize in 1981, the *Discover* Magazine Scientist of the Year Award in 1987, the NGS Centennial Award in 1988, the Westinghouse American Association for the Advancement of Science Award and the American Geological Institute Award in 1990, the U.S. Navy Robert Dexter Award for Scientific Achievement in 1992, the Hubbard Medal (NGS's highest honor), in 1996, and the American Geophysical Union Excellence in Geophysical Education Award in 1997. Ballard has 16 honorary doctorate degrees, numerous published scientific papers, and copious articles and books for the lay reader. The National Geographic Society has featured him on several television specials.

Ballard's studies of the rock composition on the continental margin of the Gulf of Maine and the Mid-Atlantic Ridge advanced the theory of plate tectonics. The finding of oases of life on the otherwise barren, basaltic seafloor supplied marine biologists and evolutionists decades' worth of new research material. His faith in undersea exploration technology that others considered simply expensive toys made possible the location and survey of dozens of historically significant shipwreck sites. Because he views the sea as the most remarkable museum one can visit, he has generously shared his discoveries with the public through awe-inspiring photographs of hidden secrets, through his spellbinding written accounts, and in real time via fiber optics from across the world. From his 1970s research in marine geology to his more recent discoveries in marine archeology and maritime history, Ballard has proven repeatedly that one who works hard, follows where his or her own curiosity leads, and does what he or she loves will be successful.

CHRONOLOGY

1942	Robert Ballard is born on June 30 in Wichita, Kansas
1959	Becomes trainee at SIO and goes on first cruise

1960	Graduates from Downey High School in California
1965	Earns bachelor of science degree in geology and chemistry from the University of California at Santa Barbara and begins graduate school in oceanography at the University of Hawaii in Honolulu
1966	Accepts position with North American Aviation's Ocean Systems Group developing missions for manned submersibles and transfers to the University of Southern California
1967	Becomes a scientific liaison officer for the U.S. Navy at WHOI
1969	Is released from naval service and starts working for WHOI, eventually becoming a tenured senior scientist
1971–72	Researches the formation of geological features in the Gulf of Maine
1973	Dives for the first time in the Mid-Atlantic Ridge as part of Project FAMOUS
1974	Receives a doctorate degree in marine geology and geophysics from the University of Rhode Island Graduate School of Oceanography and becomes assistant scientist in the geology and geophysics department at WHOI
1975	Publishes first article, "Dive into the Great Rift," of a series in *National Geographic* magazine
1977	Discovers hydrothermal vents and unique colonies of living organisms on the ocean floor of the Galápagos Rift
1979	Discovers black smokers in the East Pacific Rise
1984	Explores the nuclear submarine *Thresher* wreck site with *Argo*
1985	Explores the nuclear submarine *Scorpion* wreck site and locates the RMS *Titanic* with *Argo*
1986	Uses ROV *Jason Junior* to explore *Titanic*
1987	Publishes best-seller, *The Discovery of the* Titanic

1989	JASON Project I at Marsili Seamount and Skerki Bank. Finds *Bismarck*
1992	Identifies II sunken warships from Iron Bottom Sound (Guadalcanal)
1995	Writes autobiography, *Explorations: My Quest for Adventure and Discovery Under the Sea*
1997	Retires as senior scientist in the department of applied ocean physics and engineering and director of the Center for Marine Exploration at WHOI
1998	Opens IFE at the Mystic Aquarium in Connecticut and finds USS *Yorktown*
2000	Becomes a National Geographic Explorer-in-Residence
2002	Becomes director of the Institute for Underwater Archaeology at the University of Rhode Island Graduate School in Oceanography
2003	Uses mechanical robot *Hercules* to explore the Black Sea

FURTHER READING

Ballard, Robert D. *Adventures in Ocean Exploration: From the Discovery of the* Titanic *to the Search for Noah's Flood.* With Malcolm McConnell. Washington, D.C.: National Geographic Society, 2001. Illustrated volume of his own and others' experiences.

———. *The Discovery of the* Titanic. With Rick Archbold. New York: Warner/Madison Press Books, 1987. Ballard's own account of his successful search for the legendary sunken ocean liner.

———. *Explorations: My Quest for Adventure and Discovery Under the Sea.* With Malcolm McConnell. New York: Hyperion Press, 1995. Describes explorations leading to the discovery of exotic, deep-ocean marine life, geological evidence for plate tectonics, hot hydrothermal vents, and shipwrecks.

Hill, Christine M. *Robert Ballard: Oceanographer Who Discovered the* Titanic. Berkeley Heights, N.J.: Enslow, 1999. Standard biography written for young adults.

The JASON Project. The Jason Foundation for Education. Available online. URL: http://jasonproject.org. Accessed on January 20, 2005. Official Web site for the multidisciplinary education program started by Ballard in 1989 to bring live research and exploration to the classroom.

Mystic Aquarium Institute for Exploration. Available online. URL: http://www.ife.org. Accessed on January 20, 2005. Official Web site of the organization directed by Ballard that specializes in deep-sea research and ocean exploration.

GLOSSARY

algae   a large and diverse group of eukaryotic photosynthetic protists

Alvin   a three-person, lightweight submersible with horizontal mobility and a mechanical arm with a pincer, used for research and deep-sea exploration

ANGUS   acronym for Acoustic Navigated Geological Undersea Surveyor. A still-camera sled towed by a cable from a research ship

aqualung   a tank containing compressed air that regulates air pressure so divers can breathe underwater. Invented by Jacques-Yves Cousteau and Émile Gagnan

aquanaut   a scuba diver who lives in an underwater shelter for an extended period of time, frequently leaving to explore the underwater environment

archipelago   a group of islands

Argo   a video camera sled towed by a cable from a research ship, operated by people in a control van stationed on the research vessel with monitors for viewing real-time imagery

azoic   containing no life-forms

basalt   an iron- and magnesium-rich volcanic rock found in the ocean crust

bathymetric map   a map that shows depth measurements, particularly of the ocean

bathyscaph   a navigable diving vessel used to explore deep underwater

bathysphere   a deep-sea exploration submersible shaped like a sphere, lowered by cable from a ship

bends   *see* decompression sickness

black smokers hollow chimneys that spew superhot water rich in minerals, found at hydrothermal vents

botany the scientific study of plants

cetacean a marine mammal such as a dolphin, porpoise, or whale

chemosynthesis the formation of organic compounds using energy obtained from inorganic chemicals, such as sulfides, rather than sunlight

chemosynthetic capable of chemosynthesis

chlorophyll a green pigment that absorbs sunlight; found in chloroplasts

chlorophyta green algae

chrysophyta golden algae and diatoms

cleavage in cell biology, the series of cell divisions of a fertilized egg that results in the formation of a multicellular embryo from a single-celled zygote

commensal living in a symbiotic relationship where one organism benefits and the other one neither benefits nor is harmed

continental drift theory introduced by Alfred Wegener in 1912 stating that the continents were all once part of one supercontinent that broke apart and have been traveling over the Earth's surface ever since

continental margin the part of the seabed that borders the continents, including the shelf, slope, and rise

continental shelf edge of a continent that extends several miles past the shoreline

convection the transfer of heat by the movement of warm air or liquid to the surface of an area or object

crust the outermost layer of the Earth

cytoplasm the material within a cell that is located inside the plasma membrane but external to the nucleus

decompression sickness also called "the bends," a sometimes fatal condition with symptoms of pain, paralysis, and breathing difficulty due to the release of nitrogen bubbles in the bloodstream from a sudden decrease in pressure, as when a diver ascends too quickly

dinoflagellate a type of unicellular, eukaryotic, flagellated phytoplankton

dredging   method for collecting deep-water specimens by using a framed net or a scooping device that drags on the bottom

ecology   the study of how organisms interact with their environment

eukaryotic   having a membrane-enclosed nucleus and membrane-enclosed organelles

fathom   a unit of measure equal to about six feet (1.83 m); used in marine measurements

fertilization   the process whereby a male and female gamete fuse to form a zygote

gamete   a mature male or female germ cell, such as a sperm or an egg cell

guyot   a flat-topped undersea mountain

hermaphroditic   possessing both male and female reproductive organs

hydrographer   someone who scientifically describes and analyzes the physical conditions, boundaries, flow, and related characteristics of surface waters, as oceans, lakes, and rivers

hydrothermal vent   opening in the seafloor through which superheated water is released

ichthyologic   having to do with fish

ichthyologist   one who studies fish

igneous rock   one of three primary rock types found in Earth's crust; formed by the solidification of molten magma generated deep within the planet

Jason   an unmanned, remotely operated vehicle used for exploring the deep sea. Contains video cameras and its own motor, used for close-up inspections and controlled by an operator in a control van on a research vessel

Jim suit   a suit worn to protect divers from water pressure at great depths

luminescent   emitting light

magma   the molten material deep within the Earth's crust from which igneous rock is formed

mantle   the hot, dense solid rock between the Earth's crust and outer core

marine biology   the study of organisms that live in aquatic environments

marine geology   the study of the form and composition of the ocean basins and margins and the forces that shape them

mid-oceanic ridge   an immense underwater mountain range where the oceanic crust is being torn apart by seafloor spreading

National Oceanic and Atmospheric Administration (NOAA)   a governmental organization that researches the oceans, coasts, and atmosphere to understand and predict changes in the Earth's environment and manage its coastal and marine resources

naturalist   one who studies natural history, especially zoology or botany

nitrogen narcosis   a dangerous physiological condition in which divers feel drugged from descending too far; caused by nitrogen gas building up in their bloodstream

oceanography   the study of the oceans and related phenomena

paleomagnetism   the study of the direction of the residual magnetism in ancient rocks to learn about their historical positions

peridotite   a coarse-grained igneous rock composed mainly of olivine and various pyroxenes and amphiboles

phaeophyta   brown algae

photosynthesis   the conversion of carbon dioxide and water into organic compounds using energy from sunlight; performed by plants, algae, and some prokaryotes

photosynthetic   capable of photosynthesis

phycology   the study of algae

plankton   the tiny protists, animals, and plants that drift in the surface waters of the ocean

plate tectonics   a theory stating that the Earth's surface consists of several large separate plates that float over the globe. Explains many of the Earth's geological surface features, such as volcanoes, ocean trenches, and mountains

Plectognath   an order of fishes that have powerful jaws and teeth and bony or spiny scales, such as the triggerfish, puffer, and filefish

prokaryotic   single-celled and without a membrane-bound nucleus or other membrane-bound organelles

protist   one of the obsolete kingdoms of the five-kingdom classification system; now informally used to refer to many unicellular eukaryotes and some multicellular seaweeds and slime molds

protozoan   an animallike *protist*, such as an amoeba or paramecium, that obtains nutrients by ingesting food

pyrrophyta   division of unicellular, eukaryotic, flagellated phytoplankton including dinoflagellates; "fire algae"

rebreather   device that recycles air for aquanauts by chemically removing carbon dioxide and adding oxygen from a tank as needed

remora   a bony marine fish that attaches itself by a sucker to a shark or other fish for transportation

remotely operated vehicle (ROV)   a robot used by scientists for research and exploration

rhodophyta   red algae

rift   a valley caused by faulting of the Earth's crust

salinity   the degree of salt concentration

scuba   acronym for *s*elf-*c*ontained *u*nderwater *b*reathing *a*pparatus. Equipment used for underwater breathing

seafloor spreading   the process of tectonic plate separation and formation of new crust by the rising and hardening of magma from undersea volcanic ridges

seismic profiler   an instrument that bounces sound waves through the soft sediment and off hard rocks to obtain an image of the ocean floor

sledge   a vehicle on low runners pulled by animals, used for transporting loads across ice and snow

sounding   measuring the depth of water by use of sonar, a weighted line, or other means

subduction   a process that occurs at the junction of two tectonic plates in which the edge of one buckles beneath another into the Earth's mantle

submersible   a small, manned submarine used for research and exploration

telepresence   the use of real-time video imagery to make a remote control operator feel like he or she is at the actual site

trawling   method for catching fish by using a large tapered and flattened or conical fishing net towed along the deep sea

trench   a long, narrow valley on the ocean floor

Woods Hole Oceanographic Institution (WHOI)   a private, nonprofit, marine science research facility

zoology   the study of animals

zygote   the cell formed by the union of an egg and a sperm during sexual reproduction that develops into an embryo

FURTHER RESOURCES

Books

Ballard, Robert D. *The Eternal Darkness: A Personal History of Deep-Sea Exploration.* With Will Hively. Princeton, N.J.: Princeton University Press, 2000. Reviews 20th-century advances in ocean exploration, including the bathysphere, bathyscaph, ROVs, and more.

Byatt, Andrew, Alastair Fothergill, and Martha Holmes. *The Blue Planet: A Natural History of the Oceans.* New York: DK, 2001. Published to accompany the BBC/Discovery Channel miniseries, an introduction to the planet's oceans.

Charton, Barbara. *A to Z of Marine Scientists.* New York: Facts On File, 2003. Profiles approximately 140 marine scientists, discussing their research and contributions. Includes bibliography, cross-references, and chronology.

Dasch, E. Julius, ed. *Water: Science and Issues.* 4 vols. New York: Macmillan Reference USA, 2003. Over 300 articles with topics such as ecology, ecosystems, hydrology, fish and wildlife issues, ice, ocean science, and biographies.

Day, Trevor. *Exploring the Ocean.* 4 vols. New York: Oxford University Press, 2003. Explores various aspects of the world's oceans, including currents, tides, weather patterns, the seafloor, marine life, uses by humans, and ecological issues. Written for children and young adults.

Earle, Sylvia A. *The National Geographic Atlas of the Ocean: The Deep Frontier.* Washington, D.C.: National Geographic Society, 2001. Guide to the ocean world with stunning photographs.

Ellis, Richard. *Encyclopedia of the Sea.* New York: Alfred A. Knopf, 2000. Useful, one-volume reference source with succinct entries.

Erickson, Jon. *Marine Geology: Exploring the New Frontiers of the Ocean.* Rev. ed. New York: Facts On File, 2002. An examination of the relationships between water, its life-forms, and geological structures.

Herdman, Sir William A. *Founders of Oceanography and Their Work: An Introduction to the Science of the Sea.* New York: Longmans, Green, and Company, 1923. Resourceful work that contains information about pioneering oceanographers that is otherwise difficult to find.

Kraynak, Joe, and Kim W. Tetrault. *The Complete Idiot's Guide to the Oceans.* Indianapolis, Ind.: Alpha Books, 2003. Profiles a variety of marine creatures and habitats and describes how the world depends on the oceans for survival.

McCutcheon, Scott, and Bobbi McCutcheon. *The Facts On File Marine Science Handbook.* New York: Facts On File, 2003. Convenient resource containing a glossary of terms, short biographical profiles of celebrated biologists, a chronology of events and discoveries, and useful charts and tables.

Prager, Ellen J. *The Oceans.* With Sylvia Earle. New York: McGraw-Hill, 2000. Discusses the past, present, and future of the oceans in the context of physics, chemistry, geology, and biology.

UXL Encyclopedia of Water Science. 3 vols. Detroit: U*X*L, 2004. Covers all water science topics and issues, with sidebars and glossary.

Trujillo, Alan P., and Harold V. Thurman. *Essentials of Oceanography.* 8th ed. Upper Saddle River, N.J.: Prentice Hall, 2004. Good introductory text covering all aspects of oceanography.

Internet Resources

Bigelow Laboratory for Ocean Sciences. Available online. URL: http://www.bigelow.org. Accessed on January 20, 2005. Web site of the private, nonprofit institution. Follow education links to find further resources for a variety of subjects, including marine food webs, algal blooms, coral reef preservation, and more.

Consortium for Oceanographic Research and Education. Available online. URL: http://www.coreocean.org. Accessed on January 20, 2005. Web site for a consortium of 78 members for research and education about the ocean. Contains links for information about research and educational projects and programs.

Earth Observatory: Oceans. National Aeronautics and Space Administration. Available online. URL: http://earthobservatory. nasa.gov/Topics/oceans.html. Accessed on January 20, 2005. Freely accessible publication of NASA, with ocean images and information about the effects of the ocean on the Earth's weather and climate.

FishBase. Available online. URL: http://www.fishbase.org. Last modified on December 20, 2004. Supported by seven consortium members, this Web site contains detailed information about approximately 28,500 known fish species.

NationalGeographic.com Kids. Available online. URL: http://www. nationalgeographic.com/kids. Accessed on January 20, 2005. Contains games, activities, homework help, online maps, and fun facts about marine animals.

National Oceanic and Atmospheric Administration (NOAA). Available online. URL: http://www.noaa.gov. Last updated on January 19, 2005. Federal source for news and information concerning weather, climate, the ocean, research, satellites, the coasts, fisheries, and charting and navigation.

NOAA's Undersea Research Program. Available online. URL: http://www.nurp.noaa.gov. Accessed on January 20, 2005. Oceanography news and research performed by scientists using robots, scuba, and submarines.

OceanLink. Bamfield Marine Sciences Center. Available online. URL: http://www.oceanlink.island.net. Last updated on December 20, 2004. A resource intended for educating the public about the importance of the marine environment and its conservation.

Remarkable Careers in Oceanography: Women Exploring the Oceans. Available online. URL: http://www.womenoceanographers.org. Accessed on January 20, 2005. Sponsored by the National Science Foundation and the WHOI, this site profiles amazing women in a variety of marine science careers.

Science and Technology Focus. Office of Naval Research. Available online. URL: http://www.onr.navy.mil/focus. Last updated on April 7, 2004. Designed for use by students and teachers, this site provides information about water movement, marine habitats, marine biology, ocean water, and ocean regions. The "CyberMail" link allows students to submit questions about the ONR and its research and provides help and tips for science projects.

Scripps Institution of Oceanography. University of California–San Diego. Available online. URL: http://www.sio.ucsd.edu. Accessed on January 20, 2005. Interesting articles under "Scripps News Headlines" and "Explorations" and an informational brochure on preparing for a career in oceanography.

Woods Hole Oceanographic Institution. Available online. URL: http://www.whoi.edu. Accessed on January 20, 2005. Web site for the nonprofit research facility dedicated to research and education in oceanography. Contains links for online expeditions, news releases, marine science student profiles, and more.

Periodicals

The Biological Bulletin

Published by Marine Biological Laboratory
7 MBL Street
Woods Hole, MA 02543
Telephone: (508) 289-7428
Publishes experimental research on a wide range of biological topics, including marine life. Intended for general readership.

Discover

Published by Buena Vista Magazines
114 Fifth Avenue
New York, NY 10011
Telephone: (212) 633-4400
www.discover.com

A popular monthly magazine containing easy to understand articles on a variety of scientific topics.

Nature
The Macmillan Building
4 Crinan Street
London N1 9XW
Telephone: +44 (0)20 7833 4000
www.nature.com/nature
A prestigious primary source of scientific literature.

Oceanography
Published by The Oceanography Society
P.O. Box 1931
Rockville, MD 20849-1931
Telephone: (301) 251-7708
www.tos.org/oceanography
Promotes and chronicles all aspects of ocean science and its applications.

Oceanus
Published by Woods Hole Oceanographic Institution
Mail Stop 40
Woods Hole, MA 02543
Telephone: (508) 289-3516
http://oceanusmag.whoi.edu
An online research magazine.

Science
Published by the American Association for the Advancement of
  Science
1200 New York Avenue NW
Washington, DC 20005
Telephone: (202) 326-6417
www.sciencemag.org

One of the most highly regarded primary sources for scientific literature.

Scientific American
415 Madison Avenue
New York, NY 10017
Telephone: (212) 754-0550
www.sciam.com
A popular monthly magazine that publishes articles on a broad range of subjects and current issues in science and technology.

Societies and Organizations

American Association for the Advancement of Science (www.aaas.org) 1200 New York Avenue NW, Washington, DC 20005. Telephone: 202-326-6400

American Society of Limnology and Oceanography (www.aslo.org) ASLO Business Office, 5400 Bosque Boulevard, Suite 680, Waco, Texas 76710-4446. Telephone: (254) 399-9635

Federation of American Societies for Experimental Biology (www.faseb.org) 9650 Rockville Pike, Bethesda, Maryland 20814. Telephone: (301) 634-7000

The Oceanography Society (www.tos.org) P.O. Box 1931, Rockville, MD 20849-1931. Telephone: (301) 251-7708

INDEX